dBASE IV®

Quick Start

SUE VARNON STACY, Ph.D.
Department of Business
MiraCosta College

ANTHONY W. VARNON, D.B.A., C.P.A.
Department of Accounting and Finance
Southeast Missouri State University

RELEASE	RELEASE	RELEASE
1.1	**1.5**	**2.0**

● SOUTH-WESTERN PUBLISHING CO. ●

Editor-in-Chief: Robert E. First
Acquisitions Editor: Randy Sims
Senior Production Editor: Jean Findley
Coordinating Editor: Lisa McClary
Senior Developmental Editor: David Lafferty
Consulting Editor: Mary W. Pommert
Associate Editor: Becky E. Peveler
Associate Director/Design: Darren Wright
Production Artist: Sophia Renieris
Marketing Manager: Brian Taylor

Copyright (C) 1995

by SOUTH-WESTERN PUBLISHING CO.

Cincinnati, Ohio

ISBN: 0-538-62926-6

2 3 4 5 6 7 8 9 H 99 98 97 96 95 94

Printed in the United States of America

dBASE IV is a registered trademark of Borland International, Inc.

TO THE STUDENT

This book was prepared to give you a QUICK START for using dBASE IV®,[1] Releases 1.1, 1.5, and 2.0. The lessons assume that you have never worked with dBASE IV and give you keystroke-by-keystroke instructions for using each procedure.

Do not be misled by the small size of the book—as you complete the twenty lessons, you will learn all of the basic dBASE IV procedures for preparing database files, retrieving information from the files, and preparing reports and labels. These few pages include the same procedures taught in hundreds of pages in other books. QUICK START assumes that you prefer to learn dBASE IV by using the computer—rather than by reading about dBASE IV and the computer.

After you have completed this book, you should be able to use dBASE IV efficiently in your personal work, your school work, and your office.

Sue Varnon Stacy
Anthony W. Varnon

---

[1] dBASE IV is a registered trademark of Borland International, Inc.

CONTENTS

GETTING READY FOR *d*BASE IV

LESSON OBJECTIVES:

- Introducing dBASE IV
- Preparing to use dBASE IV
  - Load DOS
  - Format a data disk
  - Plan the file
- Getting Started with dBASE IV
  - Start dBASE IV
  - Get acquainted with the Control Center
  - Use dBASE IV menus
  - Check/Change the default directory
  - Use the F2 key
  - Exit dBASE IV
- Daily QUICK START procedures

INTRODUCING dBASE IV

dBASE IV is a program used to keep records on a computer. For example, you can use dBASE IV to keep records about students in a class. These student records can contain as many as 128 categories of information about each student.

In dBASE IV terms, the computer records are a **database file**, and this file includes the following parts:

- **Fields:** Each category of information is a field (for example, first name, last name, enrollment date, GPA).

- **Data:** The specific information within the field is data (for example, LaVonne Huter, January 12, 1990, 3.87).

- **Records:** All of the data about one person is a record (for example, all of the information about LaVonne Huter).

After you have created a database file, you can easily update the records (add or delete records, change the data), locate specific information efficiently (for example, locate all students who have a GPA above 3.0), and then prepare professional reports and labels with the information.

PREPARING TO USE dBASE IV

Before you begin working with dBASE IV, you must load DOS (the disk operating system). Also, if you plan to save your files on a floppy disk, you must format the disk you will use. As a final preparation, you will learn how to plan a database file—the file you will use as you complete this QUICK START.

LOAD DOS

To load DOS, follow these steps:

1. Be sure no disks are in the disk drives and then turn on the computer and the monitor.
2. If the screen asks you to enter the current date and time, follow the instructions below:

   If the date displayed on the screen is the current date, accept the date by pressing ↵ (the Enter key). **OR if the date is not correct,** key the current date in the format shown on the screen and then press ↵ (the Enter key).

   If the time displayed on the screen is the current time, accept the time by pressing ↵ (the Enter key). **OR if the time is not correct,** key the current time in the format shown on the screen and then press ↵ (the Enter key).

After DOS is loaded, the screen will display either a DOS prompt (for example, **C>**) or a menu of software available on your system.

FORMAT A DATA DISK

If you plan to save your work on a floppy disk, you need to format a disk for this purpose. The disk to be formatted should be a new disk or a disk that you want to erase. Follow these steps to format a data disk:

1. At the DOS prompt, key **format a:** and press ↵. (If a DOS prompt is not displayed, ask your instructor how to format the disk with your system.)
2. Following the screen instructions, insert the disk to be formatted into Drive A (the top or left drive). If the drive has a door, close it. Then press ↵ to begin formatting the disk.
3. WAIT. Formatting the disk may take a minute or longer; the screen will tell you when the formatting is complete.
4. **If the screen asks for a "Volume label,"** key your last name (using uppercase or lowercase letters) and press ↵.
5. When the screen asks if you want to format another disk, key **n** (for **N**o) and press ↵.

The screen will return to the DOS prompt or your system menu. Leave your formatted data disk in the drive throughout your dBASE IV session.

PLAN THE FILE

Before you load dBASE IV to create a database file, you should plan the file. The file plan you will follow as you complete this QUICK START is outlined and discussed below.

```
Catalog name:  STUDENTS
Catalog description:  Financial Accounting Students, Fall 1994
Filename:  BASICS
File description:  Number, name, enrollment date, GPA, transfer
```

Field Name	Field Type	Width	Decimals	Index
SS_NUM	Character	11		Y
LNAME	Character	15		N
FNAME	Character	10		N
ENRDATE	Date	8		N
GPA	Numeric	5	2	N
TRANSFER	Logical	1		N

The catalog name and description. So that you can easily find a file when you need it, you will list related files in the same catalog (a subdirectory). The catalog name can include up to eight characters, including letters, numbers, and underscores. The catalog description can include as many as 80 characters, including spaces and punctuation. The longer catalog description will help you identify the catalog contents.

The filename and description. The filename can include up to eight characters, including letters, numbers, and underscores. The file description can include as many as 65 characters, including spaces and punctuation. The longer file description will help you identify the file contents.

The fields and field names. A database file can include as many as 128 fields. The exact number of fields, however, is limited by a maximum width of 4,000 characters.

Each field name must follow these rules:

1. Maximum length: 10 characters
2. First character: a letter (A to Z)
3. Remaining characters: letters, numbers, or underscores (no other characters or punctuation; no blank spaces)

The field types. The data that you will store in each field must be described as one of the following field types:

Character: The data can include any characters.

Numeric: The data can include only numbers and a decimal, if needed. If the numbers contain a decimal, all data in the field will have the same number of decimal places. *This data type should be used only for numbers that may be calculated. That is, a telephone number or Social Security number should be described as a character field, whereas a unit price should be described as a numeric field.*

Float: The data can include only numbers and a decimal, if needed. However, if the numbers contain a decimal, the number of decimal places may be different in each item; that is, the decimal point is a **floating** decimal. *For business applications you should use the numeric field type for numbers rather than the float type.*

Date: The data can include only legitimate dates stored as MM/DD/YY (for example, 02/21/93).

Logical: The data can include only T or F (True or False) or Y or N (Yes or No).

Memo: The data can include any characters. The memo field is used for large blocks of information of variable lengths; for example, one record may include 150 characters in the memo field while another record includes 500 characters in the field.

The field widths. You must enter the width for each character field (1-254 spaces) and for each numeric and float field (1-20 spaces). dBASE IV automatically assigns the width for date fields (8 spaces), logical fields (1 space), and memo fields (10 spaces). The combined width for all fields can be no more than 4,000 spaces.

Decimal places. For each numeric field, you must assign a specific number of decimal places (0-18). The number of decimal places must be at least 2 less than the field width to leave room for the decimal and a possible minus sign for negative numbers.

Index. When you enter the records into your database file, you may enter the records in a predetermined order (for example, numerically by student number) or in no particular order. If you know that later you will want to see the records in alphabetical or numerical order according to the data in a specific field, you can make that determination at this point in your file plan. That is, you can decide whether you want an index on the field. You can index on character, numeric, float, and date fields, but not on logical or memo fields. When you want to arrange the records on two fields (for example, last name and then first name), you must create the index with a different procedure that you will learn in Lesson 5.

As a major part of your QUICK START, you will create the **Basics** file, retrieve information from the file, and prepare labels and reports with the information.

GETTING STARTED WITH dBASE IV

Getting started with dBASE IV includes starting the dBASE IV program, getting acquainted with the opening screen (the Control Center), learning to use menus, and other procedures discussed in this section. As you study the procedures, complete each step on your computer.

START dBASE IV

The procedures for starting dBASE IV depend on how the program was installed on your system. Two possible alternatives are outlined below. If neither works with your system, check with your instructor.

1. If you have not already done so, load DOS (as outlined on page 3).
2. If you have not already done so, insert a formatted data disk into the floppy disk drive.
3. Start dBASE IV:
   To start from DOS:
   A. Change to the subdirectory in which dBASE IV was installed:
      (1) At the DOS prompt, key **cd dBase** (or other subdirectory name).
      (2) Press ↵ (the Enter key).
   B. Start dBASE IV:
      (1) At the DOS prompt, key **dBase**.
      (2) Press ↵.
   OR to start from your system menu: Select: *dBASE IV*
4. If the dBASE IV Control Center does not appear quickly, respond to the screen prompt by pressing ↵.

GET ACQUAINTED WITH THE CONTROL CENTER

As soon as dBASE IV is started, the Control Center is displayed. Take time now to get acquainted with this important screen. The following sections describe the different parts of the Control Center screen.

```
┌─────────────────────────────────────────────────────────────────────────┐
│  Catalog   Tools   Exit                                   10:22:38 am     │
│                         dBASE IV CONTROL CENTER                           │
│                                                                           │
│                        CATALOG: A:\UNTITLED.CAT                           │
│                                                                           │
│      Data        Queries      Forms      Reports     Labels   Applications│
│   ┌──────────┬────────────┬──────────┬──────────┬──────────┬──────────┐   │
│   │ <create> │  <create>  │ <create> │ <create> │ <create> │ <create> │   │
│   │          │            │          │          │          │          │   │
│   │          │            │          │          │          │          │   │
│   │          │            │          │          │          │          │   │
│   │          │            │          │          │          │          │   │
│   │          │            │          │          │          │          │   │
│   │          │            │          │          │          │          │   │
│   └──────────┴────────────┴──────────┴──────────┴──────────┴──────────┘   │
│                                                                           │
│   File:        New file                                                   │
│   Description: Press ENTER on <create> to create a new file               │
│                                                                           │
│                                                                           │
│   Help:F1  Use:◄┘  Data:F2  Design:Shift-F2  Quick Report:Shift-F9  Menus:F10 │
└─────────────────────────────────────────────────────────────────────────┘
```

Catalog Tools Exit

This line at the top of the screen is the menu bar for the Control Center. You will use this menu bar when you are ready to create a new **catalog**, when you need a **tool** to tell dBASE IV where your data disk is stored, and when you are ready to **exit** the dBASE IV program at the end of your session.

A:\UNTITLED.CAT

A: identifies the default directory—where dBASE IV will look for your data disk. \ **UNTITLED.CAT** identifies the name of the catalog (file listing) that is currently open. When you start dBASE IV, the catalog that was used last will be the open catalog.

Note: The directory and catalog displayed on your screen may be different. If the named directory is not your data disk drive, you will soon use the Tools available on the menu bar to change the directory.

Data Queries Forms Reports Labels Applications

These headings and the columns below the headings are called task panels. The headings identify the various types of files you can create with dBASE IV. You will use the **<create>**

option below the heading to create a file of the specified type. When names appear below these headings, they are files that have already been created and listed in the current catalog. You can have as many as 200 files in each panel.

File: New file

Description: Press ENTER on <create> to create a new file

When **<create>** is highlighted in one of the task panels, dBASE IV tells you to begin creating a new file (as shown here). When a filename is highlighted in one of the panels, dBASE IV identifies the file in these lines.

Help:F1 Use:↵ Data:F2 Design:Shift-F2 Quick Report:Shift-F9 Menus:F10

This is the **navigation line**. The line tells you how to navigate (move) from the Control Center to other screens and menus.

USE dBASE IV MENUS

Each dBASE IV screen has a menu bar at the top. In this section you will practice opening a menu, closing a menu, selecting a menu option, and canceling a menu selection.

Open a menu with the F10 and Right Arrow keys. You can open the menu bar by pressing the F10 key. Then, if the menu you want is not open, press the Right Arrow to open the desired menu. Practice this procedure by opening the Tools menu:

> Press F10
> Press →

Close a menu. If you open a menu and then decide not to use it, close the menu by pressing the Esc (Escape) key. Practice this procedure by closing the Tools menu:

> Press Esc

Open a menu with the Alt key. You can open a menu faster by holding down the Alt key and pressing the first letter of the menu name. Practice this procedure by opening the Tools menu:

> Press Alt-T (hold down the Alt key and press the T key)

Select a menu option with an ARROW key. After a menu is open, you can select an option from the menu by highlighting the option with the Down Arrow and then pressing ↵. Practice this procedure by selecting *DOS utilities* from the Tools menu:

> Press ↓ ↓ ↓ to highlight the option (when the option is highlighted, dBASE IV explains the purpose of the option in the message line at the bottom of the screen)
> Press ↵ to select the highlighted option

Cancel a selected option. In addition to closing an open menu, you will also use the Esc key to cancel a selected menu option. Practice this procedure by canceling the *DOS utilities* option:

> Press Esc
> When you are asked if you are sure you want to
> abandon the operation, select *Yes* by pressing **Y**

Select a menu option with a letter key. You can select a menu option faster by simply pressing the first letter of the option. Practice this procedure by again selecting *DOS utilities*:

> Open the Tools menu (press Alt-T)
> Press **D**
> Cancel the selection by pressing Esc and then **Y**

CHECK/CHANGE THE DEFAULT DIRECTORY

If the directory named at the top of the Control Center is not your data disk drive, you must change the default directory by following these steps:

1. Be sure you have a formatted data disk in the disk drive.
2. Open the Tools menu.
3. Select: *DOS utilities*.
4. Open the DOS menu.
5. Select: *Set default drive:directory*.
6. Erase the current directory by pressing Ctrl-Y (hold the Ctrl key down and press the Y key).
7. Key your data disk drive (for example, **a:**) and then press ↵ (the Enter key).
8. Open the Exit menu.
9. Select: *Exit to Control Center*.

Assume that your data disk drive is not listed, and practice these steps to change the directory:

> Press Alt-T (to open the Tools menu)
> Press D (to select *DOS utilities*)
> Press Alt-D (to open the DOS menu)
> Press S (to select *Set default drive:directory*)
> Press Ctrl-Y (to erase the displayed directory)
> Key **a:** (or other drive name)
> Press ↵
> Press Alt-E (to open the Exit menu)
> Press E (to select *Exit to Control Center*)

USE THE F2 KEY

The F2 key works like a switch key. For example, if you press the Esc key from the Control Center and then select *Yes*, the Control Center will be replaced by a dot at the bottom of the screen. This is the Dot Prompt, which experienced dBASE IV operators use when they want to bypass the Control Center. When the Dot Prompt appears, you can switch back to the Control Center by pressing the F2 key. Practice this procedure now:

>From the Control Center, press ESC and then **Y**
>From the Dot Prompt, press the F2 key to switch
>   back to the Control Center

As you will soon see, the F2 key is also used to switch between the Edit screen and the Browse screen—two different ways of looking at the records in your database file.

EXIT dBASE IV

At the end of each dBASE IV session, you must exit the program correctly—otherwise you may lose part of your work. To do this, follow these steps:

1. Open the Exit menu.

2. Select: *Quit to DOS*.

Practice this procedure now:

>   Press Alt-E
>   Press **Q**

DAILY QUICK START PROCEDURES

As you work through this QUICK START, you will perform the following procedures each day:

1. Load DOS.
2. Insert your formatted data disk.
3. Start dBASE IV.
4. Check/change the default directory.
5. Complete a QUICK START lesson:
    A. Complete the lesson application.
    B. Complete the supplementary application, referring to the lesson summary as needed.
6. Exit dBASE IV.
7. Remove your data disk.

• • • • • • • • • • • • • • •

LESSON 1: *CREATING A CATALOG AND THE DATABASE FILE STRUCTURE*

LESSON OBJECTIVES:

■ Create a new catalog
■ Define the database file structure
■ Correct errors on the Database Design screen
■ Describe the database file
■ Save the database file structure
■ Exit dBASE IV

APPLICATION 1: CREATING A CATALOG AND THE DATABASE FILE STRUCTURE

In this application, you will create the following catalog and database file structure.

```
Catalog name:  STUDENTS
Catalog description:  Financial Accounting Students, Fall 1994
Filename:  BASICS
File description:  Number, name, enrollment date, GPA, transfer

File structure:

Field Name    Field Type    Width    Decimals    Index
SS_NUM        Character     11                   Y
LNAME         Character     15                   N
FNAME         Character     10                   N
ENRDATE       Date          8                    N
GPA           Numeric       5        2           N
TRANSFER      Logical       1                    N
```

CREATE A NEW CATALOG

As your first step, you will create a catalog for the student files that you will work with throughout this QUICK START.

1. Check the default directory and change it if necessary (see page 10).
2. Open the Catalog menu at the top of the Control Center by pressing Alt-C (or F10).
3. Select *Use a different catalog* by pressing **U** (or ↵ to select the highlighted option).
4. In the list at the right, *<create>* is highlighted. Select this highlighted option by pressing ↵.
5. For the catalog name, key **STUDENTS** (or **students**; dBASE IV converts all file-names to uppercase). If you make an error, press Backspace to erase the error.
6. After keying the name, press ↵.
7. Describe the files that will be listed in the catalog:
   A. Open the Catalog menu by pressing Alt-C (or F10).
   B. Select *Edit description of catalog* by pressing **E** (or ↓↓ and ↵).
   C. Key **Financial Accounting Students, Fall 1994** and then press ↵ .

DEFINE THE DATABASE FILE STRUCTURE

You are now ready to enter the database file structure.

1. In the Data panel, *<create>* is highlighted. Select this highlighted option by pressing ↵.

2. Define the first field:
   A. For the field name, key **SS_NUM** (or **ss_num**—dBASE IV converts all field names to uppercase) and then press ↵.
   B. Accept *Character* as the field type by pressing ↵. (Although you will enter Social Security numbers into this field, you will not calculate the numbers; there-fore, *character* is the correct field type.)
   C. For the field width, key **11** (using the numeral 1, not the letter l) and then press ↵.
   D. The cursor skips the decimal column because a character field does not have a set number of decimal places.
   E. To create an index on the field, change the *N* to *Y* by pressing the Spacebar; then press ↵. (An index will enable you to later arrange the records by Social Security numbers.)
3. Define the LNAME field:
   A. Key **LNAME** and press ↵.
   B. Accept *Character* by pressing ↵.
   C. Key **15** and press ↵.
   D. Accept *No* index by pressing ↵.
4. Define the FNAME field:
   A. Key **FNAME** and press ↵.
   B. Accept *Character* by pressing ↵.
   C. Key **10** and press ↵.
   D. Accept *No* index by pressing ↵.
5. Define the ENRDATE field:
   A. Key **ENRDATE** and press ↵.

B. Press the Spacebar until the field type is *Date*; then press ↵.

C. Dates are automatically 8 spaces wide for MM/DD/YY and they have no decimal places; therefore, the cursor jumps to the index column. Accept *No* index by pressing ↵.

6. Define the GPA field:
   A. Key **GPA** and press ↵.
   B. Change the field type to *Numeric* by pressing the Spacebar; then press ↵.
   C. Key **5** and press ↵.
   D. Because GPA is a numeric field, the cursor stops for the number of decimal places. Key **2** and press ↵.
   E. Accept *No* index by pressing ↵.

7. Define the TRANSFER field:
   A. Key **TRANSFER** and press ↵.
   B. Press the Spacebar until *Logical* is displayed as the field type; then press ↵. The cursor jumps to the next line because a logical field is automatically one space wide, has no decimal places, and cannot be used to index the file.

CORRECT ERRORS ON THE DATABASE DESIGN SCREEN

Before saving the file structure, you should check your work against the file plan. For practice, you will make one change in the structure. Then, if you find errors in your entries, you will correct them.

1. Change SS_NUM to SS_NO:
   A. Move up to *SS_NUM* by pressing ↑ as needed.
   B. Move to *NUM* by pressing → as needed.
   C. Erase *NUM* by pressing the Delete key three times.
   D. Key **NO** and press ↵.

2. Check your file structure and correct any additional errors, using the following keys:
   To move to the error:
   A. Move to the field: Press ↑ or ↓.
   B. Move to the column: Press Tab to move forward or Shift-Tab to move backward.
   C. Move one position left or right in the field name or width column: Press ← or →.

To correct the error:
A. Erase the current character: Press Delete.
B. Erase the preceding character: Press Backspace.
C. Erase all characters to the right in the field name or width column: Press Ctrl-Y.
D. Insert a field: Press Ctrl-N.
E. Delete a field: Press Ctrl-U.

DESCRIBE THE DATABASE FILE

To help you identify the file later, you will enter a file description.

1. Open the Layout menu by pressing Alt-L (or F10).
2. Select *Edit database description* by pressing **E** (or ↵).
3. Key **Number, name, enrollment date, GPA, transfer** and press ↵.

SAVE THE DATABASE FILE STRUCTURE

As the final step, you will save the database file structure on your data disk.

1. Open the Exit menu by pressing Alt-E (or F10 → → → →).
2. Select *Save changes and exit* by pressing **S** (or ↵).
3. For the filename, key **BASICS** (or **basics**) and press ↵.

When the Control Center is again displayed, the database filename appears above the line in the Data panel. A filename listed above the line indicates that the file is open.

COMPLETE SUPPLEMENTARY APPLICATION 1

For additional practice with the procedures covered in this lesson, complete Supplementary Application 1 on page 94. Use the lesson summary on the following page as needed.

EXIT dBASE IV

At the end of each dBASE IV session, you must exit the program correctly. Otherwise, you may lose part of your work. You will exit dBASE IV now.

1. Open the Exit menu by pressing Alt-E (or F10 → →).
2. Select *Quit to DOS* by pressing **Q**.

CREATE A NEW CATALOG   1A

Create the catalog:

Open the Catalog menu
Select: *Use a different catalog*
Select: *<create>*
Enter the catalog name (key and press ↵)

Describe the files that will be listed in the catalog:

Open the Catalog menu
Select: *Edit description of catalog*
Enter the catalog description (key and press ↵)

DEFINE THE DATABASE FILE STRUCTURE   1B

From the Data panel, select: *<create>*

Complete each field as follows:

Key the **field name**. If the field name does not
fill the column, press ↵; otherwise, the cursor will automatically jump to the next column
If the **field type** is character, press ↵; if the
field type is not character, press the
Spacebar until the correct type is displayed;
then press ↵
Key the **field width** for each character, numeric, or float field; then press ↵ if necessary to
move to the next column
Key the desired number of **decimal** places for
each numeric field; then press ↵ if necessary
to move to the next column
To create an **index** on the field data, press the
Spacebar to change the *N* to *Y*; then press ↵.
To accept *No* index, simply press ↵

CORRECT ERRORS ON THE DATABASE DESIGN SCREEN   1C

Move to the error:

Move up or down a field: Press ↑ or ↓
Move right one column: Press Tab
Move left one column: Press Shift-Tab
Move left or right one position in the field name
or width column: Press ← or →

Correct an error in the field name, field type, or
field width:

Erase the current character: Press Delete
Erase the preceding character: Press
Backspace
Erase the characters to the right: Press Ctrl-Y

Insert a field: Press Ctrl-N

Delete a field: Press Ctrl-U

DESCRIBE THE DATABASE FILE   1D

On the Database Design screen, open the Layout
menu

Select: *Edit database description*

Enter the file description (key the description and
press ↵)

SAVE THE DATABASE FILE STRUCTURE   1E

Open the Exit menu

Select: *Save changes and exit*

Enter the database filename (key and press ↵)

EXIT dBASE IV   1F

Open the Exit menu

Select: *Quit to DOS*

LESSON 2: *ENTERING RECORDS INTO THE DATABASE FILE*

LESSON OBJECTIVES:

- Open a catalog
- Enter records into the file
- Correct errors on the Edit screen
- Save the records
- Display the records
- Print a Quick Report
- Exit dBASE IV

APPLICATION 2: ENTERING RECORDS INTO THE DATABASE FILE

In this application, you will enter the following records into the Basics database file.

SS_NO	LNAME	FNAME	ENRDATE	GPA	TRANSFER
915-33-6790	Mendoza	Javier	08/21/89	3.89	T
924-33-4689	Roodman	Toby	02/09/89	3.67	F
432-22-6789	Cruse	Frances	08/21/89	3.86	F
262-47-9288	Sharp	Steve	02/09/89	3.88	T
236-44-9987	Sharp	Patt	02/09/89	3.92	T

OPEN A CATALOG

If the Students catalog is not listed at the top of the Control Center, you will open the catalog now.

1. Open the Catalog menu at the top of the Control Center (Alt-C or F10).
2. Select *Use a different catalog* (U or ↵).
3. Select the Students catalog:
   A. In the list at the right, highlight *STU-DENTS.CAT* by pressing ↓ as needed.
   B. Select the highlighted catalog by pressing ↵.

ENTER RECORDS INTO THE FILE

In this section, you will enter the five records shown at the top of this application.

If you make an error as you are keying, press Backspace to erase the error and continue keying. If you see an error made earlier, press an Arrow to move back to the error and key over it.

1. In the Data panel, highlight *BASICS*.
2. Bring up the Edit screen by pressing F2.
3. Enter the first record as follows:
   A. Key **915-33-6790** but do not press ↵. The number fills the field and the cursor jumps to the LNAME field. Your computer may also beep to let you know the field is full. (If you press ↵ by mistake, move back to the LNAME field by pressing ↑ .)
   B. Key **Mendoza** (using uppercase and lowercase as shown) and then complete the entry by pressing ↵.
   C. Key **Javier** and then complete the entry by pressing ↵.
   D. The ENRDATE field provides diagonals to separate the month, day, and year.

To enter the date, key **082189** but do not press ↵; the date fills the field and the cursor jumps to the next field.
   E. Although the GPA field displays the decimal, you will key both the numbers and the decimal. Key **3.89** but do not press ↵; the number fills the field and the cursor jumps to the next field. (If you press ↵ by mistake, the cursor will skip the last field and move to the next record; move back by pressing PgUp and then ↓ needed.)
   F. Key **T** (a transfer student); do not press ↵; the data fills the field and the cursor jumps to the next record.
4. Referring to the preceding steps as needed, enter the remaining four records shown at the top of this application.

CORRECT ERRORS ON THE EDIT SCREEN

Before saving the records, you will check your work and correct any errors.

1. Move back to the preceding record by pressing PgUp.

   Note: *If the records are not in the order you entered them, it is because you did not complete Supplementary Application 1 and/or exit dBASE IV at the end of the previous lesson. Until you close the Basics file (by opening a new file, exiting dBASE IV, or specifically closing the file), the index you created in the Basics file structure (the SS_NO index) remains active and arranges the records by Social Security numbers.*

2. Move to any error:

If you use an Arrow, Home, or End key on the numeric keypad, be sure Num Lock is off before pressing the key.

A. Move to the field: Press ↑ or ↓.
B. Move left or right one position: Press ← or →.
C. Move to the beginning of the field: Press Home.
D. Move to the end of the field: Press End.

3. Correct the error:
   A. Erase the current character: Press Delete.
   B. Erase the preceding character: Press Backspace.
   C. Erase all characters to the right: Press Ctrl-Y.
   D. Insert an additional character: Press Insert.
   E. Change back to typeover mode so that the keyed character replaces the current character: Press Insert again.

4. Continue checking the records, pressing PgUp to move to the preceding record or PgDn to move to the following record.

5. If you move past the last record in the file, you will be asked if you want to *Add new records?* Select *No*.

SAVE THE RECORDS

To save the records on your data disk, you will exit the Edit screen.

1. Open the Exit menu (Alt-E or F10 → → →).
2. Select *Exit* (E or ↵).

The Basics filename is displayed above the line in the Data panel, indicating that the file is still open.

DISPLAY THE RECORDS

You can display the records in the database file at any time. You will display the records in the Basics file.

1. With *BASICS* highlighted in the Data panel, press ↵.
2. Select *Display data*.
3. The records are available one record at a time (the Edit screen) or a screenful at a time (the Browse screen). You can switch between these two data screens by pressing F2. Press F2 now to switch to the Browse screen.

4. If all records are not displayed on the Browse screen, press PgUp.
5. Switch back to the Edit screen by pressing F2 again.
6. Return to the Control Center:
   A. Open the Exit menu.
   B. Select *Exit*.

PRINT A QUICK REPORT

You can create several kinds of reports with dBASE IV. At this point, you will print a Quick Report of the Basics file.

1. With *BASICS* highlighted in the Data panel, press Shift-F9.
2. Prevent blank pages during printing:
   A. Select *Control of printer* (C).
   B. Select *New page* (N).
   C. Change the selection to *NONE* by pressing the Spacebar.
   D. Close the submenu by pressing Esc.
3. Be sure your printer is ready. Your instructor will give you specific procedures for using the printers in your classroom.
4. Select *Begin printing* (B or ↵).

The Quick Report automatically includes the page number, the date, and a total for any numeric field (the GPA in this report).

COMPLETE SUPPLEMENTARY APPLICATION 2

For additional practice with the procedures covered in this lesson, complete Supplementary Application 2 on page 94. Use the lesson summary on the following page as needed.

EXIT dBASE IV

1. Open the Exit menu (Alt-E or F10 → →).
2. Select *Quit to DOS* (**Q**).

SUMMARY: ENTERING RECORDS INTO THE DATABASE FILE

OPEN A CATALOG   2A

At the Control Center, open the Catalog menu

Select: *Use a different catalog*

Select the desired catalog

ENTER RECORDS INTO THE FILE   2B

In the Data panel, highlight the database filename

Bring up the Edit screen by pressing F2

Enter the data for each field:

> If the data fills the field width, the cursor will automatically jump to the next field; otherwise, press ↵ after keying the data.
> **Character field:** Key all characters
> **Numeric field:** Key all numbers and any decimal—do not key commas or $
> **Date field:** Key two digits each for the month, the day, and the year—do not key the diagonals
> **Logical field:** Key **T** for true or **F** for false (or **Y** for yes, **N** for no)
> **Memo field:** (Memo fields will be discussed in Lesson 18)

After the data for the last field is entered, a new record screen will be displayed

CORRECT ERRORS ON THE EDIT SCREEN   2C

Move the cursor:

> Move to the next record: Press PgDn
> Move to the previous record: Press PgUp
> Move up or down a field: Press ↑ or ↓
> Move to the beginning of the field: Press Home
> Move to the end of the field: Press End

Correct the error:

> Erase the current character: Press Delete
> Erase the preceding character: Press Backspace
> Delete all characters to the right: Press Ctrl-Y
> Change to insert mode: Press Insert
> Change back to typeover mode: Press Insert

If you move past the last record, you will be asked if you want to Add new records? Select: No

SAVE THE RECORDS   2D

Open the Exit menu

Select: *Exit*

DISPLAY THE RECORDS   2E

At the Control Center, highlight the database filename in the Data panel

Press ↵

Select: *Display data*

Switch back and forth between the Edit screen (single-record) and the Browse screen (multiple-records) by pressing F2

If all records are not displayed on the Browse screen, press PgUp

Return to the Control Center:

> Open the Exit menu
> Select: *Exit*

PRINT A QUICK REPORT   2F

At the Control Center, highlight the database filename in the Data panel

Press Shift-F9

Prevent blank pages during printing:

> Select: *Control of printer*
> Select: *New page*
> Select: *NONE* (by pressing the Spacebar)
> Close the submenu by pressing Esc

Be sure your printer is ready

Select: *Begin printing*

EXIT dBASE IV   2G

Open the Exit menu

Select: *Quit to DOS*

LESSON 3: *EDITING THE DATABASE FILE*

• • • • • • • • • • • • • • • •

LESSON OBJECTIVES:

- ■ Display the records
- ■ Add records
- ■ Delete records
- ■ Unmark a record for deletion
- ■ Change existing records
- ■ Undo a change to a record
- ■ Save the edited file

APPLICATION 3:   *EDITING THE DATABASE FILE*

In this application, you will edit the Basics database file by adding new records, deleting records, and changing the data in existing records.

Note: *The instructions in each application assume that you completed the Supplementary Application and/or exited dBASE IV at the end of the preceding lesson. If you did not, the records may not be in the order indicated in the current application.*

DISPLAY THE RECORDS

To edit the Basics file, you will first display the records.

1. Open the Students catalog (Alt-C, U).
2. In the Data panel, highlight *BASICS*.
3. Press ↵.
4. Select *Display data* (D).

You can edit records from either the Edit screen or the Browse screen. For practice you will use both screens as you complete the editing procedures in this application.

Before you move on, locate the status bar (the highlighted line near the bottom of the screen) and observe the contents of its five sections: The first section identifies the current screen; the second section identifies the file you are working with; the third section identifies the location of the cursor; the fourth section identifies the source of the data; and the fifth section provides information about the keyboard (if NumLock or Caps is on, for example). You will see another use of the fifth section later in this application.

ADD RECORDS

You will add two new students to the Basics file.

1. Add a record on the Browse screen:
   A. If the Edit screen is displayed, switch to the Browse screen by pressing F2.
   B. Open the Records menu (Alt-R).
   C. Select *Add new records* (A).
   D. Enter the following record, pressing ↵ only when the data does not fill the field:
      423-32-6777
      Liu ↵
      Bill ↵
      112287
      3.86
      F
2. Add a record on the Edit screen:

A. Switch to the Edit screen by pressing F2.
B. Open the Records menu (Alt-R).
C. Select *Add new records* (A).
D. Enter the following record, pressing ↵ only when the data does not fill the field:
   287-88-3478
   Sharp ↵
   Bill ↵
   020989
   3.45
   F

DELETE RECORDS

To delete a record, you must complete two steps: mark the record for deletion and then erase the marked record. You will mark and then erase two records from the Basics file.

1. Mark the Mendoza record for deletion:
   A. On the Edit screen, move to the Mendoza record by pressing PgUp as needed.
   B. Open the Records menu (Alt-R or F10).
   C. Select *Mark record for deletion* (M).

*The marked record remains on the screen (and in the file), but **Del** is displayed in the last section of the status bar.*

2. Mark the Steve Sharp record for deletion:
   A. Switch to the Browse screen by pressing F2.
   B. Move to the Steve Sharp record by pressing ↓ as needed.
   C. Open the Records menu (Alt-R or F10).
   D. Select *Mark record for deletion* (M).

*The record remains on the screen, but **Del** is displayed in the status bar.*

3. Erase the two marked records from the file:
   A. Open the Organize menu (Alt-O or F10 →).
   B. Select *Erase marked records* (E).
   C. When asked if you are sure, select *Yes*.

The two records (Mendoza and Steve Sharp) are no longer in the file.

UNMARK A RECORD FOR DELETION

After you erase a record, you cannot get it back. However, if you change your mind about a marked record before you erase it, you can unmark the record.

As a shortcut, you can mark and/or unmark a record for deletion simply by moving to the record and pressing Ctrl-U. You will use this shortcut to mark and then unmark the Cruse record.

1. Move to the Cruse record by pressing ↓.
2. Mark the record for deletion by pressing Ctrl-U. *Del* is now displayed in the status bar.
3. Unmark the record by again pressing Ctrl-U. *Del* is no longer displayed in the status bar.

CHANGE EXISTING RECORDS

To change the data in an existing record, you simply move to the data you want to change and make the desired change. You will change the GPA of one student and the first name of another student.

1. On the Browse screen, change Bill Sharp's GPA to **3.72:**
   A. Move to Bill Sharp's record by pressing ↓ as needed.
   B. Move to the GPA field by pressing Tab as needed.
   C. Move to the **4** by pressing → →.
   D. Key **72** but do not press ↵ because the data fills the field.
2. On the Edit screen, change Bill Liu's first name to William:
   A. Switch to the Edit screen by pressing F2.
   B. Move to the Liu record by pressing PgUp.
   C. Move to the FNAME field by pressing ↓ ↓.
   D. Erase *Bill* by pressing Ctrl-Y.
   E. Key **William** and press ↵.

UNDO A CHANGE TO A RECORD

When you edit a record, dBASE IV automatically records the change as soon as you move the cursor to a different record. If you decide not to make the change before leaving the record, you can undo the change.

Because you have not yet moved the cursor from the Liu record, you will undo the change you just made in the first name.

1. Open the Records menu (Alt-R or F10).
2. Select *Undo change to record* (U).

Liu's first name is again ***Bill***.

SAVE THE EDITED FILE

Now that you have completed the editing, you will return to the Control Center. When you follow this procedure, dBASE IV saves any changes that have not yet been recorded.

1. Open the Exit menu (Alt-E or F10 → → → →).
2. Select *Exit* (E).

As a shortcut, you can also save the changes and return to the Control Center by pressing Ctrl-End.

COMPLETE SUPPLEMENTARY APPLICATION 3

For additional practice with the procedures covered in this lesson, complete Supplementary Application 3 on page 95. Use the lesson summary on the following page as needed.

DISPLAY THE RECORDS   3A

Open the appropriate catalog

In the Data panel, highlight the database filename

Press ↵

Select: *Display data*

ADD RECORDS   3B

On either the Edit screen or the Browse screen, open the Records menu

Select: *Add new records*

Enter the data for each field, pressing ↵ only when the data does not fill the field

DELETE RECORDS   3C

Move to the record:

On the Browse screen, press PgUp or PgDn to display the screen containing the record; then press ↓ or ↑ to move to the record
On the Edit screen, press PgUp or PgDn to move to the record

Mark a record for deletion:

Open the Records menu
Select: *Mark record for deletion*
Shortcut: Mark a record for deletion by pressing Ctrl-U.

Erase the marked record(s):

Open the Organize menu
Select: *Erase marked records*
Select: *Yes*

UNMARK A RECORD FOR DELETION   3D

Move to the record

Open the Records menu

Select: *Clear deletion mark*

Shortcut: Unmark a record for deletion by pressing Ctrl-U.

CHANGE EXISTING RECORDS   3E

Move to the record:

On the Browse screen, press PgUp or PgDn to display the screen containing the record; then press ↓ or ↑ to move to the record
On the Edit screen, press PgUp or PgDn to move to the record

Move to the data to be changed:

On the Browse screen:
Move to the field by pressing Tab (to move forward) or Shift-Tab (to move backward)
Move within the field with → or ←
On the Edit screen:
Move to the field with ↵ or ↓
Move within the field with → or ←

Make the desired changes:

Delete preceding character: Press Backspace
Delete current character: Press Delete
Delete all characters to the right: Press Ctrl-Y
Insert text: Press Insert, key the text, press Insert again
Replace text: Key the characters; the keyed text will replace the current text

Complete the change by pressing ↵

If you press ↵ on the last field of the last record, you will be asked if you want to **Add new records?** *Select:* **No**

UNDO A CHANGE TO A RECORD   3F

Before leaving the record, open the Records menu

Select: *Undo change to record*

SAVE THE EDITED FILE   3G

Open the Exit menu

Select: *Exit*

Shortcut: Press Ctrl-End

LESSON 4: *SORTING THE DATABASE FILE*

LESSON OBJECTIVES:

- Sort on a single field
- Display the sorted records
- Sort on multiple fields
- Close a database file
- Delete unneeded files

APPLICATION 4: *SORTING THE DATABASE FILE*

In this application, you will sort the student records into two different orders: first in numerical order by Social Security number and then in alphabetical order by name.

When you entered the records into the Basics file, you did not arrange them in any particular order. If you prefer to place them in a different order (for example, alphabetically by student name), you can sort the records now.

You can sort on any character, numeric, or date field. In addition, you can sort in ascending order (0-9, A-Z) or descending order (9-0, Z-A).

Finally, you can indicate if uppercase is important in the sort (an ASCII sort) or if uppercase is not important (a dictionary sort). For example, an ASCII sort would place **Zomwalt** before **deLaney**; a dictionary sort would place **deLaney** before **Zomwalt**. You should use the dictionary sort when you are sorting character fields so that names beginning with lowercase letters will be in alphabetic order—and in the event you make mistakes in entering your data.

SORT ON A SINGLE FIELD

First, you will sort the Basics file on the SS_NO field. This sort will arrange the records in numerical order by Social Security numbers, smallest numbers first.

1. Open the Students catalog.
2. Begin the sort procedure:
   A. In the Data panel, highlight *BASICS*.
   B. Press ↵.
   C. Select *Modify structure/order*.
   D. The Database Design screen is displayed with the Organize menu open. From the Organize menu, select *Sort database on field list*.
3. Identify the sort field and type of sort:
   A. Bring up the Pick list (list of field names) by pressing Shift-F1.
   B. In the list at the right, highlight *SS_NO* and press ↵.
   C. Accept *SS_NO* as the field order by again pressing ↵.
   D. *Ascending ASCII* is the displayed type of sort. This type of sort (0-9, A-Z, a-z) is appropriate for the Social Security numbers. Therefore, accept *Ascending ASCII* by pressing ↵.

E. The cursor is now on a blank line in the field order column. Indicate that the sort is complete by pressing ↵ on this blank line.
4. Name and describe the sorted file:
   A. For the new filename, key **PRIMARY** (or **primary**) and press ↵. (dBASE IV will not permit you to sort the file under the same filename.)
   B. For the file description, key **Students sorted by number** and press ↵.
5. End the sort procedure:
   A. Open the Exit menu.
   B. Select *Save changes and exit*.
   C. As requested at the bottom of the screen, confirm the exit by pressing ↵.

DISPLAY THE SORTED RECORDS

The Control Center shows that the unsorted Basics file is still open (the filename is listed above the line in the Data panel). To observe the sorted records, you will open the new Primary file and display the records.

1. In the Data panel, highlight *PRIMARY*.
2. Use a shortcut to display the records of the Primary file: Press F2. If the Edit screen is displayed, switch to the Browse screen by pressing F2 again.
3. The records in the Primary file are in ascending numerical order according to the students' Social Security numbers. After viewing the sorted records, return to the Control Center:
   A. Open the Exit menu.
   B. Select *Exit*.

SORT ON MULTIPLE FIELDS

This time you will sort the records in the Basics file by name—LNAME and then FNAME. That is, any students with the same last name will be arranged by first name.

1. Begin the sort procedure:
   A. In the Data panel, highlight *BASICS* and press ↵.

B. Select *Modify structure/order*.

C. From the Organize menu, select *Sort database on field list*.

2. Identify the LNAME field as the first sort field:

A. Bring up the Pick list by pressing Shift-F1.

B. Highlight *LNAME* and press ↵.

C. Accept *LNAME* as the field order by again pressing ↵.

D. Change the type of sort to Ascending Dictionary (0-9, Aa-Zz) by pressing the Spacebar two times.

E. Accept *Ascending Dictionary* as the type of sort by pressing ↵.

3. Identify the FNAME field as the second sort field:

A. Bring up the Pick list again by pressing Shift-F1.

B. Highlight *FNAME* and press ↵.

C. Accept *FNAME* as the field order by again pressing ↵.

D. Change the type of sort to *Ascending Dictionary* by pressing the Spacebar two times.

E. Accept *Ascending Dictionary* as the type of sort by pressing ↵.

4. Indicate that the multiple sort is complete by pressing ↵ on the blank line in the field order column.

5. Name and describe the new sorted file:

A. For the new filename, key **NAMES** and press ↵.

B. For the file description, key **Students sorted by name** and press ↵.

6. End the sort procedure:

A. Open the Exit menu.

B. Select *Save changes and exit*.

C. Confirm the exit by pressing ↵.

7. View the sorted records in the Names file:

A. In the Data panel, highlight *NAMES*.

B. Bring up the records by pressing F2.

C. The students with the same last name (Sharp) are in alphabetical order according to their first names (Bill and Patt). After viewing the sorted records, return to the Control Center by opening the Exit menu and selecting *Exit*.

CLOSE A DATABASE FILE

When you open a different database file, or when you exit dBASE IV, any open file is automatically closed. However, you can specifically close a file when you need to.

For example, in the next section you will delete the Names file, which is now open. You cannot delete an open file; therefore, you will close the Names file now.

1. With *NAMES* highlighted in the Data panel, press ↵.

2. Select *Close file*.

DELETE UNNEEDED FILES

You now have three files on your disk that include the same records. The file sorted by number—the Primary file—is the only one you want to keep. Therefore, you will delete the Names and Basics files.

1. Delete the Names file:

A. In the Data panel, highlight *NAMES*.

B. Open the Catalog menu.

C. Select *Remove highlighted file from catalog*.

D. Remove the file from the catalog by selecting *Yes*.

E. Delete the file from the data disk by again selecting *Yes*.

2. Delete the Basics file:

A. In the Data panel, highlight *BASICS*.

B. Open the Catalog menu.

C. Select *Remove highlighted file from catalog*.

D. Remove the file from the catalog by selecting *Yes*.

E. Delete the file from the data disk by again selecting *Yes*.

As you have seen, sorting a database file is a long procedure. In addition, you are left with duplicate database files on your disk. For these reasons, you will not sort the database again. Instead, when you want to see the records arranged in other orders, you will create and use indexes—a simple procedure that you will learn in the following lesson.

COMPLETE SUPPLEMENTARY APPLICATION 4

For additional practice with the procedures covered in this lesson, complete Supplementary Application 4 on page 96. Use the lesson summary on the following page as needed.

SORT ON A SINGLE FIELD   4A

In the Data panel, highlight the database filename

Press ↵

Select: *Modify structure/order*

From the Organize menu, select: *Sort database on field list*

Describe the desired sort:

> Bring up a field list by pressing Shift-F1
> Select the sort field
> Accept the displayed *Field order* by pressing ↵
> If the displayed *Type of sort* (Ascending ASCII) is not the type you want, press the Spacebar until the desired type is displayed
> Accept the displayed *Type of sort* by pressing ↵

Indicate that the sort is complete by pressing ↵ on a blank line in the *Field order* column

Enter a new filename for the sorted file

Enter the file description

Open the Exit menu

Select: *Save changes and exit*

Confirm the exit by pressing ↵

DISPLAY THE SORTED RECORDS   4B

In the Data panel, highlight the database filename

Bring up the records by pressing F2

If the Edit screen is displayed, switch to the Browse screen by pressing F2 again

If all records are not displayed on the Browse screen, press PgUp

After viewing, return to the Control Center:

> Open the Exit menu
> Select: *Exit*

SORT ON MULTIPLE FIELDS   4C

In the Data panel, highlight the database filename

Press ↵

Select: *Modify structure/order*

From the Organize menu, select: *Sort database on field list*

Describe the most important sort:

> Bring up a field list by pressing Shift-F1
> Select the most important sort field
> Accept the selected *Field order* by pressing ↵
> If the displayed *Type of sort* is not the type you want, press the Spacebar until the desired type is displayed
> Accept the displayed *Type of sort* by pressing ↵

Describe the next sort:

> Bring up a field list by pressing Shift-F1
> Select the next sort field
> Accept the selected *Field order* by pressing ↵
> If the displayed *Type of sort* is not the type you want, press the Spacebar until the desired type is displayed
> Accept the displayed *Type of sort* by pressing ↵

Indicate that the multiple-sort is complete by pressing ↵ on a blank line in the *Field order* column

Enter a new filename for the sorted file

Enter the file description

Open the Exit menu

Select: *Save changes and exit*

Confirm the exit by pressing ↵

CLOSE A DATABASE FILE   4D

In the Data panel, highlight the database filename

Press ↵

Select: *Close file*

DELETE UNNEEDED FILES   4E

In the Data panel, highlight the database filename

Open the Catalog menu

Select: *Remove highlighted file from catalog*

Select: *Yes*

When asked if you also want to remove the file from the disk, again select: *Yes*

LESSON 5: *CREATING AND USING INDEXES*

LESSON OBJECTIVES:

- Create a single-field index
- Create a multiple-field index
- Create a multiple-field index with a combination of field types
- Open an index
- Close an index

APPLICATION 5: CREATING AND USING INDEXES

In this application, you will create three indexes for the Primary database file. Each index will arrange the student records in a different order without creating a new database file.

An index is a method of temporarily arranging the database records in a particular order. You can have as many as 47 indexes for each database file.

dBASE IV automatically saves the indexes for the Primary database file in one index file named Primary.mdx. When you make changes in the database file, dBASE IV automatically updates all of the indexes.

CREATE A SINGLE-FIELD INDEX

The records in the Primary file are already sorted by Social Security numbers. However, when you add new students to the file, dBASE IV will add their records to the end of the file.

You will create an index to use each time you want to see all records in numerical order by Social Security number.

1. Open the Students catalog.
2. Display the records of the Primary file:
   A. In the Data panel, highlight *PRIMARY*.
   B. Press F2.
   C. Although you can create an index from the Edit screen, you should use the Browse screen so that you can immediately see the records in index order. Therefore, if the Edit screen is displayed, switch to the Browse screen by again pressing F2.
3. Begin the index procedure:
   A. Open the Organize menu.
   B. Select *Create new index*.
4. Identify the index field and type of sort:
   A. Select *Name of index* by pressing **N** or ↵.
   B. For the index name (up to 10 characters), key **NUMBER** and press ↵.
   C. Select *Index expression* by pressing **I** or ↵.
   D. Bring up a Pick list by pressing Shift-F1.
   E. From the fieldname column, select the highlighted *SS_NO* by pressing ↵.
   F. Accept *SS_NO* as the index expression by pressing ↵.

G. *ASCENDING* is the default order of index. This order is appropriate; therefore, you will make no change.
5. No other selections are required. Therefore, save the index by pressing Ctrl-End.

CREATE A MULTIPLE-FIELD INDEX

You will often want to see the records in alphabetical order by the students' names. (In the previous lesson, you sorted the records in this order and then deleted the sorted file.)

You will want students who have the same last name to be alphabetized by first name. Therefore, you will create a multiple-field index based on the LNAME and FNAME fields.

1. Begin the index procedure:
   A. Open the Organize menu.
   B. Select *Create new index*.
2. Identify the index fields and type of sort:
   A. Select *Name of index* by pressing **N** or ↵.
   B. For the index name, key **NAME** and press ↵.
   C. Select *Index expression* by pressing **I** or ↵.
   D. Bring up the Pick list by pressing Shift-F1.
   E. To select the first index field, highlight *LNAME* and press ↵.
   F. To add a second index field, key **+** (a plus sign).
   G. Bring up the Pick list again by pressing Shift-F1.
   H. To select the next index field, highlight *FNAME* and press ↵.
   I. Accept *LNAME+FNAME* as the index expression by pressing ↵.
3. Save the index by pressing Ctrl-End.

The new index becomes active immediately—the records are arranged in alphabetical order by last name. Students who have the same last name (Sharp) are further alphabetized by first name (Bill and Patt).

CREATE A MULTIPLE-FIELD INDEX WITH A COMBINATION OF FIELD TYPES

The third index will arrange the records first by ENRDATE (a date field) and then by LNAME and FNAME (character fields).

*When you create an index with different field types, you have to convert the non-character fields to strings (characters) in the index expression. To convert a date field to characters, key **DTOS** (date to string) before keying the field name in parentheses; for example, **DTOS(ENRDATE)**. To convert a numeric field to characters, key **STR** (string) before keying the field name in parentheses; for example, **STR(GPA)**.*

Therefore, to create a Datename index, you will enter the following index expression: **DTOS(ENRDATE)+LNAME+FNAME**.

1. Begin the index procedure:
   A. Open the Organize menu.
   B. Select *Create new index*.
2. Identify the index fields and type of sort:
   A. Select *Name of index* by pressing **N** or ↵.
   B. For the index name, key **DATENAME** and press ↵.
   C. Select *Index expression* by pressing **I** or ↵.
   D. For the index expression, key **DTOS(ENRDATE)+LNAME+FNAME** and then accept the expression by pressing ↵.
3. Save the index by pressing Ctrl-End.

The new index is now active—the records are arranged in chronological order by enrollment date. Students who enrolled on the same date are alphabetized by last name, and students with the same last name are alphabetized by first name.

Why is the top record identified in the status bar as Record 3 (Rec 3/5)? When dBASE IV rearranges the records for an index, the physical order of the records in the file does not actually change—just the order in which the records are displayed. Record 3 will be Record 3, no matter which index is active—even if the record is displayed at the top or end of the indexed file.

OPEN AN INDEX

The indexes are available to you from either the Edit screen, the Browse screen, or the Control Center. You will open one of the indexes from the Browse screen and then one from the Control Center.

1. Open the Name index from the Browse screen:
   A. Open the Organize menu.
   B. Select *Order records by index*.
   C. In the list at the right, highlight *NAME* and press ↵. The records are immediately rearranged in the new index order.
2. Open the Datename index from the Control Center:
   A. Return to the Control Center by opening the Exit menu and selecting *Exit*.
   B. From the Data panel, select the highlighted *PRIMARY* file by pressing ↵.
   C. Select *Modify structure/order*.
   D. The Organize menu is open on the screen; select *Order records by index*.
   E. Highlight *DATENAME* and press ↵.
   F. View the records in index order by pressing F2. You may need to press PgUp to display all records.
   G. Return to the Control Center by opening the Exit menu and selecting *Exit*.

CLOSE AN INDEX

You can close an index by closing the database file or by selecting a different index. When you want to see the records in the order you entered them (or later sorted them), select the Natural Order index (which is the same as no index). You will close the Datename index by selecting the Natural Order index.

1. With *PRIMARY* highlighted in the Data panel, press ↵.
2. Select *Modify structure/order*.
3. From the Organize menu, select *Order records by index*.
4. Select *Natural Order*.
5. Display the records by pressing F2. If necessary, press PgUp to display all records.

The records are now in the natural order—sorted by Social Security numbers in Lesson 4. In the natural order, Record 1 is always the top record.

*Return to the Control Center by opening the Exit menu and selecting **Exit**.*

COMPLETE SUPPLEMENTARY APPLICATION 5

For additional practice with the procedures covered in this lesson, complete Supplementary Application 5 on page 96. Use the lesson summary on the following page as needed.

SUMMARY: CREATING AND USING INDEXES

CREATE A SINGLE-FIELD INDEX 5A

In the Data panel, highlight the database filename

Display the records by pressing F2

Open the Organize menu

Select: *Create new index*

Name the index:
   Select: *Name of index*
   Enter an index name

Enter the index expression:
   Select: *Index expression*
   Bring up a field list by pressing Shift-F1
   Select the index field from the Fieldname column
   Accept the displayed *Index expression* by pressing ↵

If you want to change the index order from Ascending to Descending, select: *Order of index*

Save the index by pressing Ctrl-End

Note: An index becomes effective as soon as it is created and remains effective until another index is created or selected during the same dBASE IV session—or until the file is closed.

CREATE A MULTIPLE-FIELD INDEX 5B

Open the Organize menu

Select: *Create new index*

Name the index:
   Select: *Name of index*
   Key an index name; press ↵

Enter the index expression:
   Select: *Index expression*
   Bring up a field list by pressing Shift-F1
   Select the most important index field
   To add a second field, key **+** (a plus sign)
   Bring up the field list again by pressing Shift-F1
   Select the next index field
   Accept the displayed *Index expression* by pressing ↵

If you want to change the index order from Ascending to Descending, select: *Order of index*

Save the index by pressing Ctrl-End

Example: To index on last name and then first name, enter **LNAME+FNAME** as the index expression.

CREATE A MULTIPLE-FIELD INDEX WITH A COMBINATION OF FIELD TYPES 5C

Open the Organize menu

Select: *Create new index*

Name the index:
   Select: *Name of index*
   Enter an index name

Enter the index expression:

Select: *Index expression*

Key the index expression, converting numeric and date fields to characters, as follows: Before a numeric field, key **STR** (string) and then the field name in parentheses. Before a date field, key **DTOS** (date to string) and then the field name in parentheses

Accept the index expression by pressing ↵

Save the index by pressing Ctrl-End

Examples:
   To index on default date plus last name, enter **DTOS(DEFDATE)+LNAME** as the index expression.
   To index on amount plus last name, enter **STR(AMOUNT)+LNAME** as the index expression.
   To index on default date plus amount, enter **DTOS(DEFDATE)+STR(AMOUNT)** as the index expression.

OPEN AN INDEX 5D

To open an index from the Edit or Browse screen:

   Open the Organize menu
   Select: *Order records by index*
   Select the desired index

To open an index from the Control Center:

   In the Data panel, highlight the database filename
   Press ↵
   Select: *Modify structure/order*
   From the Organize menu, select: *Order records by index*
   Select the desired index

To view the records in the index order, press F2 (if all records are not displayed on the Browse screen, press PgUp)

To return to the Control Center (with the index still active), open the Exit menu; select: *Exit*

CLOSE AN INDEX 5E

Open a different index
OR close the database file
OR exit dBASE IV

LESSON 6: *MOVING AROUND IN THE FILE AND SEARCHING FOR INFORMATION*

LESSON OBJECTIVES:

- Move to the top or last record
- Skip a specified number of records
- Move to a specific record
- Search for specific data
- Use wildcards to search for specific data
- Search for data in an indexed field

APPLICATION 6: *MOVING AROUND IN THE FILE AND SEARCHING FOR INFORMATION*

In this application, you will move around in the Primary database file and search for specific data in the file.

MOVE TO THE TOP OR LAST RECORD

The Go To menu available on the Edit and Browse screens helps you move quickly through the database file. You will use the Go To menu to move directly to the last record in the file and then directly to the first record in the file.

1. Open the Students catalog.
2. Display the records of the Primary file (highlight *PRIMARY* in the Data panel; press F2).
3. Move directly to the last record (Roodman):
   A. Open the Go To menu.
   B. Select *Last record*.
4. Move directly to the first record (Patt Sharp):
   A. Open the Go To menu.
   B. Select *Top record*.

SKIP A SPECIFIED NUMBER OF RECORDS

To move quickly through the file, you can also skip a specified number of records. You will skip the next three records.

1. Open the Go To menu.
2. Select *Skip*.
3. Press Backspace to remove the displayed number of records.
4. For the number of records to skip, key **3** and press ↵.

The status bar shows that Record 4 (Cruse) is now the current record.

MOVE TO A SPECIFIC RECORD

When you know the number of the record you want to see, you can use the Go To menu to move directly to that record. You will move directly to Record 2, the Bill Sharp record.

1. Open the Go To menu.
2. Select *Record number*.
3. Press Backspace to remove the displayed record number.
4. For the desired record number, key **2** and press ↵.

The status bar shows that Record 2 (the Bill Sharp record) is now the current record.

SEARCH FOR SPECIFIC DATA

With the Search option on the Go To menu, you can quickly locate specific data in the file. You will search for the two Sharp (Patt and Bill) records.

1. Move the highlighting to the LNAME field by pressing Tab on the Browse screen or ↓ on the Edit screen.
2. Open the Go To menu.
3. Select *Forward search*.
4. For the search string (what you are looking for), key **Sharp** and press ↵.
5. The Patt Sharp record becomes the current record. To move to the next Sharp record, press Shift-F4.
6. The Bill Sharp record becomes the current record. To move back to the previous Sharp record, press Shift-F3.

USE WILDCARDS TO SEARCH FOR SPECIFIC DATA

When you do not know all of the characters you are searching for, you can use wildcards to represent the unknown characters.You can use **?** *to represent one unknown character and/or* ***** *to represent any number of unknown characters. For example,* **Franc?s** *in the FNAME field would locate* **Frances** *or* **Francis;** **11*** *in the ENRDATE field would locate everyone who enrolled in November of any year.*

You will use wildcards to complete three searches.

1. Search for all students who enrolled in November of any year:
   A. Move to the ENRDATE field by pressing Tab two times on the Browse screen or ↓ two times on the Edit screen.
   B. Open the Go To menu.
   C. Select *Forward search*.
   D. Erase the previous search string by pressing Backspace as needed.
   E. For the search string, key **11*** (meaning **11** followed by any characters) and press ↵.
   F. The cursor will move to the Liu record (11/22/87). Look for the next November enrollment date by pressing Shift-F4. (The cursor will remain in the Liu record because this is the only student with a November enrollment date.)

2. Search for all students who have a GPA between 3.80 and 3.89:
   A. Move to the GPA field.
   B. Open the Go To menu.
   C. Select *Forward search*.
   D. Erase the previous search string by pressing Backspace as needed.
   E. For the search string, key **3.8?** (meaning **3.8** followed by any one character) and press ↵.
   F. The cursor moves to the Cruse record (3.86). Move to the next answer by pressing Shift-F4.
   G. The cursor moves to the Liu record (3.86). Press Shift-F4 again, and the cursor returns to the Cruse record because only these two students have a GPA between 3.80 and 3.89.

3. Search for all students who have 33 as the middle part of their Social Security number:
   A. Move to the SS_NO field by pressing Shift-Tab on the Browse screen or ↑ on the Edit screen.
   B. Open the Go To menu.
   C. Select *Forward search*.
   D. Erase the previous search string by pressing Backspace as needed.
   E. For the search string, key ***-33-*** (meaning **-33-** preceded and followed by any characters) and press ↵.
   F. The cursor will move to the Roodman record (924-33-4689). Press Shift-F4 to see that no other records include -33- in the Social Security number.

Being able to search for data embedded in a field (like the preceding search for -33-) is especially useful in an address field. For example, you could find everyone who lives on Adams Street or Adams Avenue by searching for *Adams* in an ADDRESS field.

SEARCH FOR DATA IN AN INDEXED FIELD

When you do not need a wildcard, you can search much faster with an index. Although the increased speed will not be apparent with this small file, the speed difference would be great in a typically large business file.

You will use the Name index you created in the previous lesson to find a specific enrollment date in the file very quickly.

1. Open the Name index:
   A. Open the Organize menu.
   B. Select *Order records by index*.
   C. In the list at the right, highlight *NAME* and press ↵.
2. Search for Bill Liu:
   A. With the cursor anywhere, open the Go To menu.
   B. Select *Index key search*.
   C. Key **Liu** and press ↵.
3. The cursor will move directly to the Liu record. Return to the Control Center by opening the Exit menu and selecting *Exit*.

COMPLETE SUPPLEMENTARY APPLICATION 6

For additional practice with the procedures covered in this lesson, complete Supplementary Application 6 on page 97. Use the lesson summary on the following page as needed.

SUMMARY: MOVING AROUND IN THE FILE AND SEARCHING FOR INFORMATION

MOVE TO THE TOP OR LAST RECORD
6A

Display the records in the database file

From the Edit or Browse screen, open the Go To menu

To move to the top of the file, select: *Top record*

To move to the end of the file, select: *Last record*

SKIP A SPECIFIED NUMBER OF RECORDS
6B

From the Edit or Browse screen, open the Go To menu

Select: *Skip*

Erase the displayed number

Enter the number of records to skip

MOVE TO A SPECIFIC RECORD
6C

From the Edit or Browse screen, open the Go To menu

Select: *Record number*

Erase the displayed number

Enter the record number

SEARCH FOR SPECIFIC DATA
6D

Move to the field that contains the desired data:

On the Browse screen, move to the field by pressing Tab to move forward or Shift-Tab to move backward

On the Edit screen, move to the field by pressing ↑ or ↓

Open the Go To menu

Select: *Forward search* or *Backward search*

Enter a search string—the exact characters you are searching for

The cursor will jump to the first record containing the search string

To find the next record containing the search string, press Shift-F4

To find the previous record containing the search string, press Shift-F3

USE WILDCARDS TO SEARCH FOR SPECIFIC DATA
6E

On the Edit or Browse screen, move to the field that contains the desired data

Open the Go To menu

Select: *Forward search* or *Backward search*

Enter a search string—the exact characters you are looking for, plus one or more wildcards

To find the next record containing the search string, press Shift-F4

To find the previous record containing the search string, press Shift-F3

Examples of search strings with wildcards:

To find Tang or Tange, enter **Tang***
To find Felice or Felise, **Feli?e**
To find any number containing 3, enter ***3***
To find any number between 100 and 199, enter **1??**

SEARCH FOR DATA IN AN INDEXED FIELD
6F

Open the index:

Open the Organize menu
Select: *Order records by index*
Select the desired index

Perform the search:

With the cursor anywhere, open the Go To menu
Select: *Index key search*
Enter the search string—the exact characters you are looking for, with no wildcards

LESSON 7: *SELECTING RECORDS BY CHARACTER DATA*

• • • • • • • • • • • • • •

LESSON OBJECTIVES:

- Open the database file
- Bring up the Query Design screen
- Select records by character data—exact match
- Return to the Query Design screen
- Clear an unwanted condition
- Select records by character data—using like
- Select records by character data—using sounds like
- Select records by character data—unequal match
- Select records by embedded character data
- Exit the Query Design screen without saving the query

APPLICATION 7: SELECTING RECORDS BY CHARACTER DATA

In this application, you will select specific records from the Primary file by using the Query Design screen. You will select the records based on data in character fields.

When you need information from a few records, the Go To menu you used in the previous lesson will be very useful. However, when you need information that includes several records, or when you want to print the answers, you will use the Query Design screen to select the records you need.

OPEN THE DATABASE FILE

In previous lessons you opened the database file by displaying the data. To begin this lesson, you need the file open with the Control Center displayed. Therefore, you will use a new procedure to open the Primary file and remain at the Control Center.

1. Open the Students catalog.
2. In the Data panel, highlight *PRIMARY*.
3. Press ↵.
4. Select *Use file*.

The Control Center is displayed with the name of the open file listed above the line in the Data panel.

BRING UP THE QUERY DESIGN SCREEN

Next you will bring up the Query Design screen and observe its contents.

1. With the Primary file open, move to the Queries panel by pressing →.
2. Select the highlighted <create> by pressing ↵.

*The Query Design screen includes a **file skeleton** at the top and a **view skeleton** at the bottom. Both of these skeletons currently include the fields from the database file.*

In the next several lessons, you will learn to use these skeletons to perform the following tasks:

***File skeleton.** Select the records you need and arrange the selected records in a specific order.*

***View skeleton.** Select and arrange the fields you want to see.*

SELECT RECORDS BY CHARACTER DATA— EXACT MATCH

You can select records according to data in character, numeric, date, or logical fields. In the remainder of this lesson, you will select records based on data in character fields.

When you are searching for character data, key the search string (what you are looking for) enclosed in quotation marks. You will begin by selecting the records of all students whose last name is Sharp.

1. The highlighting is currently under the filename (*Primary.dbf*) in the file skeleton. The data you are looking for is in the LNAME field (called the **condition** field). Move the highlighting to the LNAME field by pressing Tab two times.
2. To select the records of all students named Sharp, key **"Sharp"** (including the quotation marks) and press ↵.
3. Apply the query (that is, perform the search) by pressing F2. The Patt and Bill Sharp records are displayed. The displayed data is called a view.

RETURN TO THE QUERY DESIGN SCREEN

Now that you have viewed the selected records, you will return directly to the Query Design screen to search for other information.

1. Open the Exit menu.
2. Select *Transfer to Query Design*.

CLEAR AN UNWANTED CONDITION

When you return to the Query Design screen from the view, the previous condition is still displayed in the file skeleton. Before you begin a new search, you will clear any unwanted condition.

With the highlighting on "Sharp," clear the condition by pressing Ctrl-Y.

SELECT RECORDS BY CHARACTER DATA— USING LIKE

*When you are looking for data in a character field but are not sure of the exact characters, you can use **like** and one or more wildcards to represent the unknown character(s). You can use the wildcard * to represent a group of unknown characters and/or the wildcard ? to represent a single unknown character. You will use **like** and wildcards to perform two searches.*

1. Select the records of students whose first name is like Franc?s:
   A. Move to the FNAME field by pressing Tab.
   B. For the search condition, key **like "Franc?s"** and press ↵.
   C. Apply the query by pressing F2. The Frances Cruse record is displayed.
   D. Return to the Query Design screen by opening the Exit menu and selecting *Transfer to Query Design.*
2. Select the records of students whose last name is like R*dman:
   A. Clear the previous condition by pressing Ctrl-Y.
   B. Move back to the LNAME field by pressing Shift-Tab.
   C. For the search condition, key **like "R*dman"** and press ↵.
   D. Apply the query by pressing F2. The Roodman record is displayed.
   E. Return to the Query Design screen by opening the Exit menu and selecting *Transfer to Query Design.*

SELECT RECORDS BY CHARACTER DATA—USING SOUNDS LIKE

*When you are looking for data in a character field, you can also use **sounds like** to select the records. You will select the records of students whose last name sounds like "Cruz."*

1. Clear the previous condition by pressing Ctrl-Y.
2. For the search condition, key **sounds like "Cruz"** in the LNAME field and press ↵.
3. Apply the query by pressing F2. The Frances Cruse record is displayed.
4. Return to the Query Design screen by opening the Exit menu and selecting *Transfer to Query Design.*

SELECT RECORDS BY CHARACTER DATA— UNEQUAL MATCH

Another type of search is the unequal match—that is, select all records that do not match the search string. To search for an unequal match in a character field, key # before the search string. You will select the records of all students whose last name is not Sharp.

1. Clear the previous condition.
2. For the search condition, key **#"Sharp"** in the LNAME field and press ↵.
3. Apply the query by pressing F2. All students except Bill and Patt Sharp are displayed (Liu, Cruse, and Roodman).
4. Return to the Query Design screen by opening the Exit menu and selecting *Transfer to Query Design.*

SELECT RECORDS BY EMBEDDED CHARACTER DATA

*A final type of character search is the search for data embedded in a character field. To search for embedded data in a character field, key $ before the search string. You will search for the records of all students who have **33** embedded in their Social Security number.*

1. Clear the previous condition.
2. Move back to the SS_NO field by pressing Shift-Tab.
3. For the search condition, key **$"33"** and press ↵.
4. Apply the query by pressing F2. The Roodman record is displayed.
5. Return to the Query Design screen by opening the Exit menu and selecting *Transfer to Query Design.*

EXIT THE QUERY DESIGN SCREEN WITHOUT SAVING THE QUERY

When you are through looking for information in your file, you are ready to return to the Control Center. At this point you can save the last query you created or you can abandon it. In this lesson, you will abandon the query.

1. Open the Exit menu.
2. Select *Abandon changes and exit.*
3. When asked if you are sure you want to abandon the operation, select *Yes.*

COMPLETE SUPPLEMENTARY APPLICATION 7

For additional practice with the procedures covered in this lesson, complete Supplementary Application 7 on page 97. Use the lesson summary on the following page as needed.

OPEN THE DATABASE FILE   7A

Open the catalog
In the Data panel, highlight the database filename
Press ↵
Select: *Use file*

BRING UP THE QUERY DESIGN SCREEN   7B

With the database file open, move to the Queries
   panel
Select: *<create>*
If you try to create a query before opening a database file, the Query Design screen will be displayed with the Layout menu open. Before you
   can proceed, you will have to open the database file from the Layout menu:
   From the Layout menu, select: *Add file to query*
   Select the database file from the displayed file list

SELECT RECORDS BY CHARACTER DATA— EXACT MATCH   7C

In the file skeleton at the top of the Query Design
   screen, move the highlighting to the condition
   field:
   To move forward, press Tab
   To move backward, press Shift-Tab
Enter the exact characters you are looking for,
   surrounded by quotation marks
Apply the query by pressing F2

Example: To select all Cooper records, enter
"Cooper" in the LNAME field.

RETURN TO THE QUERY DESIGN SCREEN   7D

Open the Exit menu
Select: *Transfer to Query Design*

CLEAR AN UNWANTED CONDITION   7E

With the highlighting on the unwanted condition,
   press Ctrl-Y

SELECT RECORDS BY CHARACTER DATA— USING LIKE   7F

In the file skeleton, move to the condition field
Enter **like** followed in quotation marks by the
   known characters plus one or more wildcards

Apply the query

Wildcards:
   * = any group of unspecified characters
   ? = a single unspecified character
Examples: To select all Woodman records, you
   can enter **like "*dman"** or **like "Woodm?n"** or
   like "W*dm?n" in the LNAME field.

SELECT RECORDS BY CHARACTER DATA— USING SOUNDS LIKE   7G

In the file skeleton, move to the condition field
Enter **sounds like** followed in quotation marks by
   characters that sound like the characters you
   want to find
Apply the query

Example: To select all Watters records, you can
   enter **sounds like "Waters"** in the LNAME
   field.

SELECT RECORDS BY CHARACTER DATA— UNEQUAL MATCH   7H

In the file skeleton, move to the condition field
Enter **#** followed in quotation marks by the char-
   acters you do not want to match
Apply the query

Example: To select the records of everyone
   whose last name is not **Cooper**, enter
   #"Cooper" in the LNAME field.

SELECT RECORDS BY EMBEDDED CHARACTER DATA   7I

In the file skeleton, move to the condition field
Enter **$** followed in quotation marks by the
   embedded characters you want to match
Apply the query

Example: To select the records of everyone
   whose loan number includes **45**, enter **$"45"**
   in the LOAN_NO field.

EXIT THE QUERY DESIGN SCREEN WITHOUT SAVING THE QUERY   7J

Open the Exit menu
Select: *Abandon changes and exit*
Select: *Yes*

LESSON 8: *SELECTING RECORDS BY NUMERIC DATA, DATES, OR LOGICAL DATA*

LESSON OBJECTIVES:

- Select records by numeric data—exact match
- Select records by numeric date—using relational operators
- Select records by dates—exact match
- Select records by dates—using relational operators
- Select records by logical data
- Count the records which meet the conditions
- Return directly to the Control Center without saving the query

APPLICATION 8: *SELECTING RECORDS BY NUMERIC DATA, DATES, OR LOGICAL DATA*

In this application, you will select records from the Primary file by searching for numeric data, dates, and logical data.

SELECT RECORDS BY NUMERIC DATA—EXACT MATCH

To select records that are an exact match to a number you are looking for, simply enter the number in the condition field. You will select the records of students whose GPA is 3.86.

1. Bring up the Query Design screen:
   A. Open the Students catalog.
   B. Open the Primary file (highlight *PRI-MARY*, ↵, select *Use file*).
   C. From the Queries panel, select *<create>*.
2. In the file skeleton, enter the search condition:
   A. Move quickly to the GPA field by pressing End (to move to the last field) and then Shift-Tab (to move back to the GPA field).
   B. To select all students whose GPA is 3.86, key **3.86** (no quotation marks around numeric data) and press ↵.
3. Apply the query by pressing F2. The Liu and Cruse records are displayed.
4. Return to the Query Design screen by opening the Exit menu and selecting *Transfer to Query Design*.

SELECT RECORDS BY NUMERIC DATA—USING RELATIONAL OPERATORS

In addition to an exact match, you can search for numeric data that is greater than, less than, or not equal to a specified number. To perform these and similar searches in a numeric field, key one of the following relational operators before the search string:

Relational operators:

=	Equals
>	Greater than
>=	Greater than or equal to
<	Less than
<=	Less than or equal to
<>	Not equal to

You will use the relational operators to perform two numeric searches.

1. Select the records of students whose GPA is greater than 3.80:
   A. Clear the previous condition by pressing Ctrl-Y.
   B. For the search condition, key **>3.80** in the GPA field and press ↵.
   C. Apply the query by pressing F2. The Patt Sharp, Liu, and Cruse records are displayed.
   D. Return to the Query Design screen by opening the Exit menu and selecting *Transfer to Query Design*.
2. Select the records of students whose GPA is less than or equal to 3.72:
   A. Clear the previous condition by pressing Ctrl-Y.
   B. For the search condition, key **<=3.72** in the GPA field and press ↵.
   C. Apply the query by pressing F2. The Bill Sharp and Roodman records are displayed.
   D. Return to the Query Design screen by opening the Exit menu and selecting *Transfer to Query Design*.

SELECT RECORDS BY DATES—EXACT MATCH

To select records that are an exact match to a date, enter the date enclosed in braces { } in the condition field. You will select the records of students who enrolled on February 9, 1989.

1. Clear the previous condition by pressing Ctrl-Y.
2. Move back to the ENRDATE field by pressing Shift-Tab.
3. To select students who enrolled on February 9, 1989, key **{02/09/89}** (including the braces) and press ↵.
4. Apply the query by pressing F2. The Patt Sharp, Bill Sharp, and Roodman records are displayed.
5. Return to the Query Design screen by opening the Exit menu and selecting *Transfer to Query Design*.

SELECT RECORDS BY DATES—USING RELATIONAL OPERATORS

You can also use the relational operators to search a date field. You will search for the records of students who enrolled before 1989.

1. Clear the previous condition by pressing Ctrl-Y.
2. To select students who enrolled before 1989, key **<{01/01/89}** in the ENRDATE field and press ↵.
3. Apply the query by pressing F2. The Liu record will be displayed.
4. Return to the Query Design screen by opening the Exit menu and selecting *Transfer to Query Design.*

SELECT RECORDS BY LOGICAL DATA

To select a record that matches logical data, enter T or F (or Y or N) enclosed by periods (for example, .T. or .F.). You will select the records of all non-transfer students.

1. Clear the previous condition by pressing Ctrl-Y.
2. Move directly to the TRANSFER field by pressing End.
3. To select the non-transfer students, key **.F.** and press ↵.
4. Apply the query by pressing F2. The Bill Sharp, Liu, Cruse, and Roodman records are displayed.
5. Return to the Query Design screen by opening the Exit menu and selecting *Transfer to Query Design.*

COUNT THE RECORDS THAT MEET THE CONDITIONS

Rather than display all records that meet a specified condition, you can simply count the number of records that

meet the condition. You will count the number of non-transfer students.

1. Keeping the condition in the TRANSFER field, move back to the FNAME field by pressing Shift-Tab as needed (any other field would also be all right).
2. To count the number of non-transfer students, key **count** in the FNAME field and press ↵.
3. Apply the query by pressing F2. The view displays **4** in the FNAME field to show that four students are non-transfer students. All other fields are empty.

RETURN DIRECTLY TO THE CONTROL CENTER WITHOUT SAVING THE QUERY

Rather than transfer to the Query Design screen, you can return directly to the Control Center. When you choose this exit, dBASE IV will ask if you want to save the query for later use. In this lesson, you will return to the Control Center without saving the query.

1. From the view (the answers to the query), open the Exit menu.
2. Select *Exit.*
3. When dBASE IV informs you that the Query design has been changed and asks if you want to save it, select *No.*

COMPLETE SUPPLEMENTARY APPLICATION 8

For additional practice with the procedures covered in this lesson, complete Supplementary Application 8 on page 98. Use the lesson summary on the following page as needed.

SUMMARY: SELECTING RECORDS BY NUMERIC DATA, DATES, OR LOGICAL DATA

SELECT RECORDS BY NUMERIC DATA—EXACT MATCH 8A

Open the database file:

  In the Data panel, highlight the database file-
    name
  Press ↵
  Select: *Use file*

From the Queries panel, select: *<create>*

In the file skeleton, move to the condition field

Enter the exact number you want to match (no quotation marks, commas, or $)

Apply the query by pressing F2

Example: To select all records that include an amount of $10,000, enter **10000** in the AMOUNT field.

SELECT RECORDS BY NUMERIC DATA— USING RELATIONAL OPERATORS 8B

In the file skeleton, move to the condition field

Enter a relational operator followed by a number (no quotation marks, commas, or $)

Apply the query

Relational operators:

  = Equals
  > Greater than
  >= Greater than or equal to
  < Less than
  <= Less than or equal to
  <> Not equal to

Example: To select all records that include an amount less than $10,000, enter **<10000** in the AMOUNT field.

SELECT RECORDS BY DATES—EXACT MATCH 8C

In the file skeleton, move to the condition field

Enter the exact date you want to match, enclosed in braces { }

Apply the query

Example: To select the loans that defaulted on January 1, 1993, enter **{01/01/93}** in the DEF-DATE field.

SELECT RECORDS BY DATES—USING RELATIONAL OPERATORS 8D

In the file skeleton, move to the condition field

Enter a relational operator followed by the date enclosed in braces { }

Apply the query

Example: To select the records of all loans defaulted after June 1, 1992, enter **>{06/01/92}** in the DEFDATE field.

SELECT RECORDS BY LOGICAL DATA 8E

In the file skeleton, move to the condition field

Enter the condition (T or F, or Y or N) enclosed by periods

Apply the query

Example: To select the records of all secured loans, enter **.T.** in the SECURED field.

COUNT THE RECORDS WHICH MEET THE CONDITIONS 8F

Enter the condition(s) in the file skeleton, as usual

Enter **count** in any other field of the file skeleton

Apply the query

Example: To determine the number of secured loans, enter **.T.** in the SECURED field and **count** in any other field.

RETURN DIRECTLY TO THE CONTROL CENTER WITHOUT SAVING THE QUERY 8G

Open the Exit menu

Select: *Exit*

When you are asked if you want to save the Query design, select: *No*

LESSON 9: *SELECT RECORDS USING MULTIPLE CONDITIONS AND SUMMARY CALCULATIONS*

LESSON OBJECTIVES:

- Select records with multiple conditions in different fields
- Select records with multiple conditions in the same field
- Select records with one condition or another
- Calculate records
- Calculate and count records

APPLICATION 9: SELECTING RECORDS USING MULTIPLE CONDITIONS AND SUMMARY CALCULATIONS

In this application, you will select Primary file records that meet more than one condition. You will also calculate information in selected records.

SELECT RECORDS WITH MULTIPLE CONDITIONS IN DIFFERENT FIELDS

You will often need records that must meet more than one condition. When the multiple conditions involve different fields, enter the conditions on the same line of the file skeleton. You will select the records of students who are not transfer students AND who have a GPA greater than 3.75.

1. Bring up the Query Design screen:
   A. Open the Students catalog.
   B. Open the Primary file (highlight PRIMARY, ↵, select *Use file*).
   C. From the Queries panel, select *<create>*.
2. Enter the first search condition:
   A. Tab to the GPA field.
   B. To select students with a GPA greater than 3.75, key **>3.75** and press ↵.
3. Enter the second search condition:
   A. Tab to the TRANSFER field.
   B. To select non-transfer students, key **.F.** and press ↵.
4. Apply the query by pressing F2. The Liu and Cruse records are displayed.
5. Return to the Query Design screen by opening the Exit menu and selecting *Transfer to Query Design*.

SELECT RECORDS WITH MULTIPLE CONDITIONS IN THE SAME FIELD

When multiple conditions involve the same field, separate the conditions with a comma. You will select the records of non-transfer students who have a GPA greater than 3.70 AND less than 3.90.

1. Keeping the condition in the TRANSFER field, move back to the GPA field by pressing Shift-Tab.
2. Clear the condition in the GPA field by pressing Ctrl-Y.
3. To select the non-transfer students whose GPA is greater than 3.70 and less than 3.90, key **>3.70,<3.90** and press ↵.
4. Apply the query by pressing F2. The Bill Sharp, Liu, and Cruse records are displayed.

5. Return to the Query Design screen by opening the Exit menu and selecting *Transfer to Query Design*.

SELECT RECORDS WITH ONE CONDITION OR ANOTHER

When the records you need are based on one condition OR another, enter the conditions on different lines of the file skeleton. You will perform two searches in which the records must meet one condition or another.

1. Select the records of students named Sharp or Roodman:
   A. Clear the previous conditions in the GPA and TRANSFER fields.
   B. Move back to the LNAME field by pressing Shift-Tab as needed.
   C. For the first search condition, key **"Sharp"** and press ↵. (Remember, character data must be enclosed in quotation marks.)
   D. Open a second line in the file skeleton by pressing ↓. The highlighting will be immediately below "Sharp."
   E. For the second search condition, key **"Liu"** and press ↵.
   F. Apply the query by pressing F2. The Patt Sharp, Bill Sharp, and Liu records are displayed.
   G. Return to the Query Design screen by opening the Exit menu and selecting *Transfer to Query Design*.
2. Select the records of students who either enrolled after June 1, 1989 or have a GPA greater than 3.90:
   A. Clear the previous conditions in the LNAME field.
   B. Tab to the first line of the ENRDATE field.
   C. For the first search condition, key **>{06/01/89}** and press ↵. (Remember, dates must be enclosed in braces.)
   D. Open a second line in the file skeleton by pressing ↓.

E. Tab to the GPA field.

F. For the second search condition, key **>3.90** and press ↵.

G. Apply the query by pressing F2. The records of Patt Sharp (GPA greater than 3.90) and Cruse (enrollment date after June 1, 1989) are displayed.

H. Return to the Query Design screen by opening the Exit menu and selecting *Transfer to Query Design*.

CALCULATE RECORDS

You can also calculate numeric data by entering one of the following summary operators in the field you want to calculate:

Summary operators:

avg = average
sum = add
max = largest value
min = smallest value

You will calculate the average GPA of all non-transfer students.

1. Clear the previous conditions from the file skeleton.

2. Enter the summary operator:
   A. Move to the GPA field, staying on the first line of the file skeleton.
   B. To calculate the average GPA, key **avg** and press ↵.

3. Enter the search condition:
   A. Tab to the TRANSFER field.
   B. To base the calculation on non-transfer students, key **.F.** and press ↵.

4. Apply the query by pressing F2. The view displays **3.78** in the GPA field. This is the average GPA of all non-transfer students. All other fields are empty.

5. Return to the Query Design screen by opening the Exit menu and selecting *Transfer to Query Design*.

CALCULATE AND COUNT RECORDS

*When you need to calculate a numeric field AND count the number of records that meet the specified conditions, enter the appropriate summary operator in the field to be calculated and **count** in any other field. You will calculate the average GPA of non-transfer students and count the number of non-transfer students.*

1. The summary operator in the GPA field (avg) and the search condition in the TRANSFER field (.F.) are appropriate for this query; therefore, you will not clear these entries.

2. Count the number of records being averaged:
   A. Move to the ENRDATE field (however, any other field could be used).
   B. Key **count** and press ↵.

3. Apply the query by pressing F2. The ENRDATE field shows that you have four non-transfer students; the GPA field shows 3.78 as the average GPA of these students. All other fields are empty.

4. Return directly to the Control Center without saving the query:
   A. Open the Exit menu.
   B. Select *Exit*.
   C. When asked if you want to save the query, select *No*.

COMPLETE SUPPLEMENTARY APPLICATION 9

For additional practice with the procedures covered in this lesson, complete Supplementary Application 9 on page 99. Use the lesson summary on the following page as needed.

SUMMARY: SELECTING RECORDS USING MULTIPLE CONDITIONS AND SUMMARY CALCULATIONS

SELECT RECORDS WITH MULTIPLE CONDITIONS IN DIFFERENT FIELDS
9A

Open the database file:

In the Data panel, highlight the database filename
Press ↵
Select: *Use file*

From the Queries panel, select: *<create>*

In the condition field, enter the first condition

Move to the next condition field, staying on the same line of the file skeleton

Enter the next condition

Apply the query

Example: To select the records of all unsecured loans in excess of $10,000, enter the conditions as shown:

AMOUNT	SECURED
>10000	**.F.**

SELECT RECORDS WITH MULTIPLE CONDITIONS IN THE SAME FIELD
9B

In the condition field, key the first condition, a comma, and then the next condition

Press ↵

Apply the query

Example: To select the records of all loans between $5,000 and $10,000, enter the conditions as shown:

AMOUNT
>5000,<10000

SELECT RECORDS WITH ONE CONDITION OR ANOTHER
9C

In the condition field, enter the first condition

Move down to the next line of the file skeleton by pressing ↓

In the condition field, enter the next condition

Apply the query

Example: To select the records of loans that defaulted before June 1, 1992, OR that have an amount of $12,000 or more, enter the conditions as shown:

DEFDATE	AMOUNT
<{06/01/92}	
	>=12000

CALCULATE RECORDS
9D

Enter the condition(s) in the file skeleton, as usual

Also in the file skeleton, enter the appropriate summary operator in the field you want to calculate

Apply the query

Summary operators:

avg = average
sum = add
max = largest value
min = smallest value

Example: To calculate the sum of all secured loans, complete the file skeleton as follows:

AMOUNT	SECURED
sum	**.T.**

CALCULATE AND COUNT RECORDS
9E

Enter the condition(s) in the file skeleton, as usual

Also in the file skeleton, enter the appropriate summary operator in the field you want to calculate

Enter **count** in any other field of the file skeleton

Apply the query

Example: To count the number of unsecured loans and calculate their average amounts, complete the file skeleton as follows:

LNAME	AMOUNT	SECURED
count	**avg**	**.F.**

When this query is applied, the view will show only the number of unsecured loans and their average amount; all other fields will be empty.

LESSON 10: *CREATING AND USING QUERY FILES*

LESSON OBJECTIVES:

- Begin the query file
- Select the desired records
- Arrange the records with an index
- Select the desired fields
- Describe and save the query file
- Display the query data (the view)
- Print a Quick Report of the query data
- Close a query file

APPLICATION 10: *CREATING AND USING QUERY FILES*

In this application, you will create and save a query file to select and arrange data from the Primary file. Then you will print a report with the query file.

In the previous lessons, you used the Query Design screen to select specific records from the Primary file. In this lesson, you will create a query file that will do all of the following:

• *Select the records of all non-transfer students*

• *Arrange the selected records chronologically by enrollment date*

• *Display only these fields: ENRDATE, FNAME, LNAME, and GPA*

Then you will save the query file and use it to prepare a report.

BEGIN THE QUERY FILE

1. Open the Students catalog.
2. Open the Primary file (highlight *PRIMARY*, ↵, select *Use file*).
3. From the Queries panel, select *<create>*.

SELECT THE DESIRED RECORDS

As your first step in designing the query file, you will select the records of all non-transfer students.

1. In the file skeleton, move directly to the TRANSFER field by pressing End.
2. To select the non-transfer students, key **.F.** and press ↵.
3. Check your record selection by pressing F2. The view will show the non-transfer students in this order: Bill Sharp, Liu, Cruse, and Roodman.
4. Return to the Query Design screen to continue designing the query file:
   A. Open the Exit menu.
   B. Select *Transfer to query design*.

ARRANGE THE RECORDS WITH AN INDEX

Your second step will be to arrange the records according to enrollment dates and names. To do this, you will select the Datename index created in Lesson 5.

1. Open the Fields menu.
2. Select *Include indexes*.
3. The symbol preceding the SS_NO field (# or ▲) indicates that you have an index on this

field. The multiple-field indexes are displayed at the end of the field list—LNAME+FNAME and DTOS(ENRDATE)+LNAME+FNAME. To see the last index, press End.

4. For this query file, select the index based on enrollment date and name:
   A. With the highlighting in the DTOS(ENRDATE)+LNAME+FNAME column, open the Fields menu.
   B. Select *Sort on this field*.
   C. Select *Ascending ASCII*. *Asc1* is displayed to show the selected index.
5. Check your record arrangement by pressing F2. The view will show the non-transfer students in chronological order by enrollment date (those with the same enrollment date are in alphabetical order by name): Liu, Roodman, Bill Sharp, and Cruse.
6. Return to the Query Design screen to continue designing the query file:
   A. Open the Exit menu.
   B. Select *Transfer to Query Design*.

SELECT THE DESIRED FIELDS

Your last step in designing this query file is to select the four fields you want to see, in this order: ENRDATE, FNAME, LNAME, and GPA.

In the file skeleton, the ↓ preceding each field indicates that the field is included in the view skeleton at the bottom of the screen.

The view skeleton determines the fields you will see when you apply the query. Currently the view includes all fields, arranged in the order they appear in the database file. The right arrow at the end of the field list (the lower right corner of the screen) indicates that more fields are listed at the right.

First you will delete all fields from the view skeleton; then you will select the fields you want to see.

1. Delete all fields from the view skeleton:
   A. In the file skeleton, move directly to the filename (*Primary.dbf*) by pressing Home.
   B. Delete all fields from the view skeleton by pressing F5 (for Releases 1.5 and 2.0, press F5 a second time).

2. Select the desired fields in the desired order:
   A. In the file skeleton, move to the ENR-DATE field.
   B. Select the field for the view by pressing F5.
   C. Move to the FNAME field; select the field by pressing F5.
   D. Move to the LNAME field; select the field by pressing F5.
   E. Move to the GPA field; select the field by pressing F5.
3. To practice deleting a field from the view, delete the GPA field: With the highlighting still in the GPA field, delete the field from the view by pressing F5 again.
4. Reinsert the GPA field into the view: With the highlighting still in the GPA field, select the field by pressing F5 again.
5. Check your final query file by pressing F2. The view will include the non-transfer students, arranged by enrollment date and name (Liu, Roodman, Bill Sharp, and Cruse), with only the selected fields displayed (ENRDATE, FNAME, LNAME, and GPA).
6. Return to the Query Design screen:
   A. Open the Exit menu.
   B. Select *Transfer to Query Design*.

DESCRIBE AND SAVE THE QUERY FILE

You will need this query file in the following sections. Therefore, you will describe the query and then save it on your data disk.

1. Describe the query:
   A. On the Query Design screen, open the Layout menu.
   B. Select *Edit description of query*.
   C. Key **Non-transfer students** and press ↲.
2. Save the query:
   A. Open the Exit menu.
   B. Select *Save changes and exit*.
   C. For the query name, key **NON_TRAN** and press ↲.

DISPLAY THE QUERY DATA (THE VIEW)

After you create and save a query file, you can use the query each time you want to view the selected, arranged data. You will view the Non_Tran data.

1. With *NON_TRAN* highlighted in the Queries panel, press F2.
2. If all of the selected records are not displayed (Liu, Roodman, Bill Sharp, and Cruse), press PgUp.
3. Return to the Control Center by opening the Exit menu and selecting *Exit*.

PRINT A QUICK REPORT OF THE QUERY DATA

You will now print a Quick Report of the Non_Tran data.

1. With **NON_TRAN** highlighted in the Queries panel, press Shift-F9.
2. Prevent blank pages during printing:
   A. Select *Control of printer*.
   B. Select *New page*.
   C. Change the selection to *NONE* by pressing the Spacebar.
   D. Close the submenu by pressing Esc.
3. Be sure your printer is ready.
4. Select *Begin printing*.

CLOSE A QUERY FILE

You are finished with the query file for now. Therefore, you will close the view.

1. With *NON_TRAN* highlighted in the Queries panel, press ↲.
2. Select *Close view*.

When you exit dBASE IV with a query file open, the query is automatically closed. You completed the procedure here just for practice.

COMPLETE SUPPLEMENTARY APPLICATION 10

For additional practice with the procedures covered in this lesson, complete Supplementary Application 10 on page 99. Use the lesson summary on the following page as needed.

BEGIN THE QUERY FILE 10A

Open the database file:

>In the Data panel, highlight the database file-
>name
>Press ↵
>Select: *Use file*
>From the Queries panel, select: *<create>*

SELECT THE DESIRED RECORDS 10B

In the file skeleton, enter the condition(s) for the record selection

ARRANGE THE RECORDS WITH AN INDEX 10C

Open the Fields menu

Select: *Include indexes*

Select an index:

>In the file skeleton, move the highlighting to the
>desired index field
>Open the Fields menu
>Select: *Sort on this field*
>Select the type of sort

SELECT THE DESIRED FIELDS 10D

Delete all fields from the view skeleton:

>In the file skeleton, move the highlighting to the
>filename
>Press F5 (for Releases 1.5 and 2.0, press F5 a
>second time)

Select each desired field for the view:

>In the file skeleton, move the highlighting to the
>field
>Press F5

To delete a specific field from the view:

>In the file skeleton, move the highlighting to the
>field
>Press F5

To reinsert a deleted field into the view:

>In the file skeleton, move the highlighting to the
>field
>Press F5

DESCRIBE AND SAVE THE QUERY FILE 10E

Describe the file:

>On the Query Design screen, open the Layout
>menu
>Select: *Edit description of query*
>Enter the query description

Save the file:

>Open the Exit menu
>Select: *Save changes and exit*
>Enter the query name

DISPLAY THE QUERY DATA (THE VIEW) 10F

In the Queries panel, highlight the query name

Press F2

Return to the Control Center:

>Open the Exit menu
>Select: *Exit*

PRINT A QUICK REPORT OF THE QUERY DATA 10G

In the Queries panel, highlight the query name

Press Shift-F9

Prevent blank pages during printing:

>Select: *Control of printer*
>Select: *New page*
>Select: *NONE* (by pressing the Spacebar)
>Close the submenu by pressing Esc

Be sure your printer is ready

Select: *Begin printing*

CLOSE A QUERY FILE 10H

In the Queries panel, highlight the query name

Press ↵

Select: *Close view*

LESSON 11: *CREATING A COLUMN REPORT FROM A QUICK LAYOUT*

LESSON OBJECTIVES:

- ▪ Open the appropriate query file
- ▪ Begin a column report from a Quick Layout
- ▪ Insert/delete lines and text
- ▪ Change the left margin
- ▪ View the report on the screen
- ▪ Print the report from the Report Design screen
- ▪ Describe and save the report file

APPLICATION 11: *CREATING A COLUMN REPORT FROM A QUICK LAYOUT*

In this application, you will create the following column report for the Primary file, using one of dBASE IV's Quick Layouts.

```
Current date


                NON-TRANSFER STUDENTS


    ENRDATE       FNAME       LNAME          GPA

    11/22/87      Bill        Liu            3.86
    02/09/89      Bill        Sharp          3.72
    02/09/89      Toby        Roodman        3.67
    08/21/89      Francis     Cruse          3.86
```

The Quick Report you printed in the preceding lesson does not permit you to make any changes in the report content or format. As you will see in this lesson, you can use dBASE IV's Quick Layouts to create a report that more exactly meets your needs.

OPEN THE APPROPRIATE QUERY FILE

The report you will create in this application includes only non-transfer students, arranged chronologically by enrollment dates. Also, the report includes only the ENRDATE, FNAME, LNAME, and GPA fields.

You have already saved this record selection, record arrangement, and field selection in the Non_Tran query file. Therefore, you will open the query for this report.

1. Open the Students catalog.
2. In the Queries panel, highlight *NON_TRAN*.
3. Press ↵.
4. Select *Use view*.

NON_TRAN *is now displayed above the line in the Queries panel, indicating that the query is open.*

BEGIN A COLUMN REPORT FROM A QUICK LAYOUT

dBASE IV provides a Quick Layout for three types of reports. In this lesson, you will use a Quick Layout to create a column report (a report that arranges the data in columns like a table). First you will bring up the Report Design screen and observe its contents.

1. At the Control Center, move to the Reports panel by pressing → as needed.

2. Select the highlighted <*create*> by pressing ↵.
3. From the Layout menu already open on the screen, select *Quick layouts*.
4. Select *Column layout*.

The Report Design screen is displayed with the following bands (report areas):

Page Header Band: *What will appear at the top of each report page. (The default is the page number, the date, and the field names.)*

Report Intro Band: *What will appear at the top of the first page only. (The default is no introduction.)*

Detail Band: *What will appear in the body of the report. (The default is the fields selected in the query file. When no query file is open, the default is all database fields.)*

Report Summary Band: *What will appear at the end of the last page only. (The default is a total for each numeric field.)*

Page Footer Band: *What will appear at the bottom of each report page. (The default is no footer.)*

You can change, erase, or add to any of these report bands. You will practice some of these changes as you create this first report.

INSERT/DELETE LINES AND TEXT

In the Page Header Band, you will insert blank lines and the report title. Then you will delete the Report Summary Band.

1. The cursor is currently on the line identifying the Page Header Band. Press ↓ to move into the band, immediately above the Page No.

2. Insert two more blank lines above the Page No. by pressing Ctrl-N two times.
3. Because your report will be only one page, delete the page number:
    A. Move to the Page No. line by pressing ↓ as needed.
    B. Delete the line by pressing Ctrl-Y.
4. Move below the date (MM/DD/YY) by pressing ↓.
5. Make room for the report title by inserting five blank lines above the field names: Press Ctrl-N five times.
6. Enter the report title:
    A. Move down to Line 6 (as shown in the status bar at the bottom of the screen) by pressing ↓ two times.
    B. Move into position for the title by pressing → until the cursor is in Column 12, as shown in the status bar.
    C. Key **NON-TRANSFER STUDENTS** but do not press ↵ (pressing ↵ would open another blank line, which is not needed).
7. You do not want to total the GPA field; therefore, delete the Report Summary Band:
    A. Move into the Report Summary Band by pressing ↓ as needed—to the line that shows only the total for the GPA column (*9999.99*).
    B. Delete this line by pressing Ctrl-Y.

CHANGE THE LEFT MARGIN

If you use the current print settings, your report will begin printing in the first column on the paper. For this report, you will increase the left margin by changing the page dimensions.

1. Open the Print menu.
2. Select *Page dimensions*.
3. Select *Offset from left*.
4. Delete the current setting by pressing Ctrl-Y.
5. For a new left margin, key **15** and press ↵.
6. Return to the Report Design screen by pressing Esc two times.

VIEW THE REPORT ON THE SCREEN

Before printing the report, you will check the format and content on the screen.

1. Open the Print menu.
2. Select *View report on screen*.
3. Continue viewing by pressing the Spacebar until you see the end of the report (the message "Press any key to continue").
4. Return to the Report Design screen by pressing any key.

PRINT THE REPORT FROM THE REPORT DESIGN SCREEN

You can print a report from either the Report Design screen or the Control Center. You will print this report from the Report Design screen.

1. Open the Print menu.
2. Prevent blank pages during printing:
    A. Select *Control of printer*.
    B. Select *New page*.
    C. Change the selection to *NONE* by pressing the Spacebar.
    D. Close the submenu by pressing Esc.
3. Be sure your printer is ready.
4. Select *Begin printing*.

DESCRIBE AND SAVE THE REPORT FILE

You will enter a report description to help you identify the file later. Then you will save the report file on your data disk.

1. Describe the report file:
    A. Open the Layout menu.
    B. Select *Edit description of report*.
    C. Key **Non-transfer students** and press ↵.
2. Save the report file:
    A. Open the Exit menu.
    B. Select *Save changes and exit*.
    C. For the filename, key **NON_TRAN** and press ↵.
    D. When asked if you want to save the print form settings, select *Yes* and then accept the displayed filename by pressing ↵.

COMPLETE SUPPLEMENTARY APPLICATION 11

For additional practice with the procedures covered in this lesson, complete Supplementary Application 11 on page 100. Use the lesson summary on the following page as needed.

OPEN THE APPROPRIATE QUERY FILE   11A

In the Queries panel, highlight the query name

Press ↵

Select: *Use view*

BEGIN A COLUMN REPORT FROM A QUICK LAYOUT   11B

With a database file or a query open, move to the Reports panel

Select: *<create>*

From the Layout menu, select: *Quick layouts*

Select: *Column layout*

INSERT/DELETE LINES AND TEXT   11C

Use Arrow keys to move the cursor to the desired position

To insert a line, press Ctrl-N or ↵

To delete a line, press Ctrl-Y

To insert text, key the text

To delete the current character, press Delete

To delete the preceding character, press Backspace

Note: dBASE IV will not permit you to delete a blank line at the end of a report band.

CHANGE THE LEFT MARGIN   11D

Open the Print menu

Select: *Page dimensions*

Select: *Offset from left*

Erase the current setting by pressing Ctrl-Y

Enter the new setting

Return to the Report Design screen by pressing Esc two times

VIEW THE REPORT ON THE SCREEN   11E

Open the Print menu

Select: *View report on screen*

To see the next page, press the Spacebar

To cancel the viewing, press Esc

After viewing, press any key

PRINT THE REPORT FROM THE REPORT DESIGN SCREEN   11F

Open the Print menu

Prevent blank pages during printing:

    Select: *Control of printer*
    Select: *New page*
    Select: *NONE* (by pressing the Spacebar)
    Close the submenu by pressing Esc

Be sure your printer is ready

Select: *Begin printing*

DESCRIBE AND SAVE THE REPORT FILE   11G

Describe the report:

    Open the Layout menu
    Select: *Edit description of report*
    Enter the report description

Save the report file:

    Open the Exit menu
    Select: *Save changes and exit*
    Enter the report name
    To save the print form settings; select: *Yes*; then
        accept the displayed filename by pressing ↵

LESSON 12: *CREATING A COLUMN REPORT FROM SCRATCH*

LESSON OBJECTIVES:

- Open an index from the Control Center
- Begin a column report from scratch
- Insert the current date
- Enter the report title and column headings
- Add fields
- Create a calculated field
- Insert a summary calculation
- View the report on the screen
- Describe and save the report file

APPLICATION 12: CREATING A COLUMN REPORT FROM SCRATCH

In this application, you will create the following column report from scratch. The report includes four fields from the Primary file and one field that dBASE IV calculates for you (the target GPA).

```
(Current date)

                          TARGET GPA REPORT

ENROLLMENT DATE     LAST NAME         FIRST NAME    GPA       TARGET GPA

11/22/87            Liu               Bill          3.86      3.94
02/09/89            Roodman           Toby          3.67      3.74
02/09/89            Sharp             Bill          3.72      3.79
02/09/89            Sharp             Patt          3.92      4.00
08/21/89            Cruse             Frances       3.86      3.94
                                      AVERAGE       3.81
```

OPEN AN INDEX FROM THE CONTROL CENTER

This report includes all records in the Primary file. Therefore, you do not need a query for record selection. However, you do need the Datename index to arrange the records by enrollment date and student name. You will open the Datename index from the Control Center.

1. Open the Students catalog.
2. In the Data panel, highlight *PRIMARY* and press ↵.
3. Select *Modify structure/order*.
4. From the Organize menu, select *Order records by index*.
5. In the index list, highlight *DATENAME* and press ↵.
6. Open the Exit menu.
7. Select *Save changes and exit*.
8. Confirm the exit by pressing ↵.

BEGIN A COLUMN REPORT FROM SCRATCH

Rather than use a Quick Layout, you will begin this column report from scratch.

1. With the Primary file open, move to the Reports panel and select *<create>*.
2. Close the Layout menu by pressing Esc.

INSERT THE CURRENT DATE

To include the current date each time you print the report, you will insert a predefined date in the Page Header Band.

1. Move into the Page Header Band by pressing ↓.
2. Move to Line 5 (as shown in the status bar) by pressing ↵ five times.
3. Move to Column 5 (as shown in the status bar) by pressing → five times.
4. Insert the predefined date field:
   A. Open the Fields menu.
   B. Select *Add field*.
   C. Move to the PREDEFINED column by pressing → two times.
   D. Select *Date* by pressing ↵.
   E. Return to the Report Design screen by pressing Ctrl-End.

ENTER THE REPORT TITLE AND COLUMN HEADINGS

Next you will complete the Page Header Band by entering the report title and column headings.

1. Enter the report title:
   A. Move to Line 8 by pressing ↵ three times.
   B. Move to Column 31 by pressing → as needed.
   C. Key **TARGET GPA REPORT**.
2. Enter the column headings:
   A. Move down to Line 10 by pressing ↵ two times.
   B. On Line 10, press → as needed to move to the specified column and key the following headings:

   Column 5:   **ENROLLMENT DATE**
   Column 23:   **LAST NAME**
   Column 41:   **FIRST NAME**
   Column 54:   **GPA**
   Column 61:   **TARGET GPA**

ADD FIELDS

The Detail Band is the report area that contains the field data. For this report, you will add four fields from the Primary file to the Detail Band.

1. Move into the Detail Band by pressing ↓ as needed.
2. Add the ENRDATE field:
   A. Move to Column 5.
   B. Open the Fields menu.
   C. Select *Add field*.
   D. Select the highlighted *ENRDATE* by pressing ↵.
   E. Return to the Report Design screen by pressing Ctrl-End.
3. Repeat the steps to add these fields to the Detail Band:
   Column 23:   LNAME field
   Column 41:   FNAME field
   Column 54:   GPA field

CREATE A CALCULATED FIELD

The TARGET GPA is the current GPA plus a two percent improvement. You will create this calculated field by entering this calculation expression: GPA*1.02 (the current GPA x 102%).

1. Create the calculated field:
   A. In the Detail Band, move to Column 64.
   B. Open the Fields menu.
   C. Select *Add field*.
   D. Move to the CALCULATED column and select *<create>*.
   E. Select *Name* by pressing **N**.
   F. For the field name, key **TARGETGPA** and press ↵.
   G. Select *Expression* by pressing **E**.
   H. For the calculation expression, key **GPA*1.02** and press ↵.
2. Change the field template (the way the data will be displayed in the report):
   A. Select *Template* by pressing T.
   B. The current template contains too many characters (no GPA is this long). Delete this template by pressing Backspace as needed.
   C. For the new template, key **99.99** and press ↵.
3. Return to the Report Design screen by pressing Ctrl-End.

INSERT A SUMMARY CALCULATION

The Report Summary Band is used to calculate the data in the report columns. You will insert a summary calculation to average the GPA data.

1. Move into the Report Summary Band by pressing ↓ two times.
2. For the summary heading, move to Column 33 and key **AVERAGE**.
3. Average the GPA field:
   A. Move to Column 54.
   B. Open the Fields menu.
   C. Select *Add field*.
   D. Move to the SUMMARY column.
   E. Select *Average*.
   F. Select *Field to summarize on* by pressing F.
   G. For the field to average, select *GPA*.
4. Change the field template to be the same as the GPA template on the Report Design screen (*99.99*):
   A. Select *Template* by pressing T.
   B. Delete the current template by pressing Backspace as needed.
   C. For the new template, key **99.99** and press ↵.
5. Return to the Report Design screen by pressing Ctrl-End.

VIEW THE REPORT ON THE SCREEN

Before saving the report, you will check the format and content on the screen.

1. Open the Print menu.
2. Select *View report on screen*.
3. Following the screen instructions, press the Spacebar to continue viewing.
4. Return to the Report Design screen by pressing any key.

DESCRIBE AND SAVE THE REPORT FILE

1. Open the Layout menu and select *Edit description of report*.
2. Key **Target GPA by enrollment date** and press ↵.
3. Open the Exit menu and select *Save changes and exit*.
4. Key **TARGET_GPA** and press ↵.

COMPLETE SUPPLEMENTARY APPLICATION 12

For additional practice with the procedures covered in this lesson, complete Supplementary Application 12 on page 101. Use the lesson summary on the following page as needed.

SUMMARY: CREATING A COLUMN REPORT FROM SCRATCH

OPEN AN INDEX FROM THE CONTROL CENTER 12A

In the Data panel, highlight the database filename
Press ↵
Select: *Modify structure/order*
From the Organize menu, select: *Order records by index*
Select the index
Open the Exit menu
Select: *Save changes and exit*
Confirm the exit by pressing ↵

BEGIN A COLUMN REPORT FROM SCRATCH 12B

With a database file or a query open, move to the Reports panel
Select: *<create>*
Close the Layout menu by pressing Esc

INSERT THE CURRENT DATE 12C

Move the cursor into position for the date by pressing ↵ and/or Arrow keys as needed
Open the Fields menu
Select: *Add field*
Move to the PREDEFINED column
Select: *Date*
Return to the Report Design screen by pressing Ctrl-End

ENTER THE REPORT TITLE AND COLUMN HEADINGS 12D

In the Page Header Band, move the cursor into position by pressing ↵ and/or Arrow keys as needed
Key the text

ADD FIELDS 12E

In the Detail Band, move to the desired column by pressing ← or → as needed
Open the Fields menu
Select: *Add field*
Select the field
To change the Template:
Select: *Template*
Replace the current template with the desired template
Press ↵
Return to the Report Design screen by pressing Ctrl-End

CREATE A CALCULATED FIELD 12F

In the Detail Band, move to the desired column by pressing ← or → as needed
Open the Fields menu
Select: *Add field*
Move to the CALCULATED column
Select: *<create>*
Select: *Name*
Enter the field name
Select: *Expression*
Enter the desired calculation expression
Select: *Template*
Replace the current template with the desired template and press ↵
Return to the Report Design screen by pressing Ctrl-End

INSERT A SUMMARY CALCULATION 12G

In the Report Summary Band, move the cursor into position
Open the Fields menu
Select: *Add field*
Move to the SUMMARY column
Select the desired calculation
Select: *Field to summarize on*
Select the field you want to calculate
Select: *Template*
Replace the current template with the desired template and press ↵
Return to the Report Design screen by pressing Ctrl-End

VIEW THE REPORT ON THE SCREEN 12H

Open the Print menu
Select: *View report on screen*
To continue the view, press the Spacebar
To cancel the view, press Esc
Return to the Report Design screen by pressing any key

DESCRIBE AND SAVE THE REPORT FILE 12I

Open the Layout menu
Select: *Edit description of report*
Enter the report description
Open the Exit menu
Select: *Save changes and exit*
Enter the report name

LESSON 13: *CREATING A FORM REPORT FROM A QUICK LAYOUT*

LESSON OBJECTIVES:

- Open the appropriate query file
- Begin a form report from a Quick Layout
- Add lines and text to the Page Header Band
- Move fields
- Change the report page length
- View the report on the screen
- Describe and save the report file
- Print the report from the Control Center

APPLICATION 13: CREATING A FORM REPORT FROM A QUICK LAYOUT

In this application, you will use a Quick Layout to create the following form report for each non-transfer student in the Primary file.

```
Page No.   1
(Current Date)

              NON-TRANSFER STUDENT REPORT


FNAME     Bill                    LNAME     Sharp


GPA       3.72                    ENRDATE   02/09/89
```

A form report lists the selected data for each record in any arrangement you choose. You can print a page full of records with this layout; or you can print each record on a separate report page, as you will do in this application.

OPEN THE APPROPRIATE QUERY FILE

For this report, you need the record selection, index, and field selection already saved in the Non_Tran query file. Therefore, as your first step you will open this query.

1. Open the Students catalog.
2. In the Queries panel, highlight *NON_TRAN* and press ⏎.
3. Select *Use view*.

NON_TRAN *is now displayed above the line in the Queries panel, indicating that the query is open.*

BEGIN A FORM REPORT FROM A QUICK LAYOUT

You can create a form report either from a Quick Layout or from scratch. To save time, you will use a Quick Layout for this form report.

1. With the Non_Tran query open, move to the Reports panel and select <create>.
2. From the Layout menu already open on the screen, select *Quick layouts*.
3. Select *Form layout*.

As shown on the screen, the Quick Layout for a form report includes the following:

Page Header Band: *Page number and current date.*

Detail Band: *The field names and data from the query file (or from the database file when a query is not open).*

You can change any of the report bands to meet your needs.

ADD LINES AND TEXT TO THE PAGE HEADER BAND

To improve the appearance of the report, you will insert blank lines above the page number and then enter a report title. You will make these changes in the Page Header Band.

1. Move into the Page Header Band by pressing ↓.
2. Insert five blank lines by pressing ⏎ five times.
3. Move to the end of the date by pressing ↓ ↓ and then End.
4. Move to Line 9 (as shown in the status bar) by pressing ⏎ two times.
5. Move to Column 20 by pressing → as needed.
6. For the report title, key **NON-TRANSFER STUDENT REPORT** (do not press ⏎ because you do not want to open an unneeded line).

MOVE FIELDS

As shown on the screen, the Quick Layout for a form report places all of the field names and data at the left margin. You can move the names and data to any location you choose. The procedure includes selecting the material you want to move and then moving it.

You will move the enrollment date and the last name to the locations shown in the report at the top of this application.

1. Select the ENRDATE field name and data:
   A. Move into the Detail Band by pressing ↓ as needed.
   B. Move to the beginning of ENRDATE (Line 1, Column 0).
   C. Begin the selection by pressing F6.
   D. Move to the end of the field data (Column 16) by pressing → as needed.

E. Complete the selection by pressing ↵.
2. Move the selected field name and data:
   A. Begin the move by pressing F7.
   B. Move the shaded rectangle (representing the width of the selected text) to Column 40, Line 4, by pressing → and then ↓ as needed.
   C. Complete the move by pressing ↵.
3. Select the LNAME field name and data:
   A. Move to the beginning of LNAME (Line 3, Column 0).
   B. Begin the selection by pressing F6.
   C. Move to the end of the field data (Column 23) by pressing → as needed.
   D. Complete the selection by pressing ↵.
4. Move the selected field name and data:
   A. Begin the move by pressing F7.
   B. Move the shaded rectangle to Column 40, Line 2, by pressing → and then ↑ as needed.
   C. Complete the move by pressing ↵.

CHANGE THE REPORT PAGE LENGTH

The current page length is 66 lines. With this page length, each record prints below the previous record, filling a standard-size report page. To print each student's report on a separate page, you will change the page length to 17 lines.

1. Open the Print menu.
2. Select *Page dimensions*.
3. Select *Length of page*.
4. Delete the current page length by pressing Ctrl-Y.
5. Key **17** and press ↵.
6. Close the submenu by pressing Esc.

VIEW THE REPORT ON THE SCREEN

Before saving the report, you will check the format and content on the screen.

1. From the Print menu, select *View report on screen*.

2. Move through the four-page report (one page each for Liu, Roodman, Bill Sharp, and Cruse) by pressing the Spacebar as needed.
3. Return to the Report Design screen by pressing any key.

DESCRIBE AND SAVE THE REPORT FILE

1. Open the Layout menu and select *Edit description of report*.
2. Key **Non-transfer form report** and press ↵.
3. Open the Exit menu and select *Save changes and exit*.
4. Key **TRA_FORM** and press ↵.
5. To save the print form settings, select *Yes* and then accept the displayed filename by pressing ↵.

PRINT THE REPORT FROM THE CONTROL CENTER

You can print a report from the Report Design screen or from the Control Center. You will print this report from the Control Center.

1. In the Reports panel, highlight *TRA_FORM* and press ↵.
2. Select *Print report*.
3. Prevent blank pages during printing:
   A. Select *Control of printer*.
   B. Select *New page*.
   C. Change the selection to *NONE* by pressing the Spacebar.
   D. Close the submenu by pressing Esc.
4. Be sure your printer is ready.
5. Select *Begin printing*.

COMPLETE SUPPLEMENTARY APPLICATION 13

For additional practice with the procedures covered in this lesson, complete Supplementary Application 13 on page 102. Use the lesson summary on the following page as needed.

SUMMARY: CREATING A FORM REPORT FROM A QUICK LAYOUT

OPEN THE APPROPRIATE QUERY FILE · 13A

In the Queries panel, highlight the query name

Press ↵

Select: *Use view*

BEGIN A FORM REPORT FROM A QUICK LAYOUT · 13B

With a database file or a query open, move to the Reports panel

Select: *<create>*

From the Layout menu, select: *Quick layouts*

Select: *Form layout*

ADD LINES AND TEXT TO THE PAGE HEADER BAND · 13C

Move the cursor into the Page Header Band

Insert desired blank lines by pressing Ctrl-N or ↵ as needed

Add text:
    Move to the desired position by pressing Arrow keys as needed
    Key the text

MOVE FIELDS · 13D

Select the field name and/or data to be moved:
    Move the cursor to the beginning of the field name and/or data to be moved
    Press F6
    Highlight the field name and/or data by pressing →
    Complete the selection by pressing ↵

Move the selected field name and/or data:
    Press F7
    Move the highlighted rectangle to the desired location
    Complete the move by pressing ↵

CHANGE THE REPORT PAGE LENGTH · 13E

Open the Print menu

Select: *Page dimensions*

Select: *Length of page*

Delete the current length by pressing Ctrl-Y

Enter the desired page length

Close the submenu by pressing Esc

Return to the Report Design screen by pressing Esc

VIEW THE REPORT ON THE SCREEN · 13F

Open the Print menu

Select: *View report on screen*

To continue the view, press the Spacebar

To cancel the view, press Esc

Return to the Report Design screen by pressing any key

DESCRIBE AND SAVE THE REPORT FILE · 13G

Open the Layout menu

Select: *Edit description of report*

Enter the report description

Open the Exit menu

Select: *Save changes and exit*

Enter the report name

To save the print form settings; select: *Yes*; then accept the displayed filename by pressing ↵

PRINT A REPORT FROM THE CONTROL CENTER · 13H

In the Reports panel, highlight the report name

Press ↵

Select: *Print report*

Prevent blank pages during printing:
    Select: *Control of printer*
    Select: *New page*
    Select: *NONE* (by pressing the Spacebar)
    Close the submenu by pressing Esc

Be sure your printer is ready

Select: *Begin printing*

LESSON 14: *CREATING A MAILMERGE REPORT FROM A QUICK LAYOUT*

LESSON OBJECTIVES:

- Begin a mailmerge report from a Quick Layout
- Set margins and tabs
- Create a calculated field for side-by-side data
- Enter a paragraph into a mailmerge report
- Add fields
- Use special text styles
- View the report on the screen
- Print the report from the Report Design screen
- Describe and save the report file

APPLICATION 14: *CREATING A MAILMERGE REPORT FROM A QUICK LAYOUT*

In this application, you will use a Quick Layout to create the following mailmerge report for each student in the Primary file.

```
TO:       (FNAME and LNAME fields from the Primary file)

FROM:     Patrick Sebrechts, Instructor

DATE:     February 20, 1994

SUBJECT:  Accounting Club Scholarship

Now that the grade reports have been completed for this
semester, I look forward to discussing the possibilities of
an Accounting Club Scholarship with you.

Your current grade point average of (GPA field) is certainly
commendable and will earn you a great deal of consideration.
```

BEGIN A MAILMERGE REPORT FROM A QUICK LAYOUT

You need this report for each student in the Primary file. Therefore, you do not need a query to select records. You will open the database file and begin a mailmerge report from a Quick Layout.

1. Open the Students catalog and the Primary file.
2. From the Reports panel, select <create>.
3. Select *Quick layouts*.
4. Select *Mailmerge layout*.

The mailmerge Quick Layout leaves only the Detail Band open. This area is like a blank sheet of paper for your document.

SET MARGINS AND TABS

The ruler at the top of the screen shows the left margin ([) at 0 inches. The current tab settings are shown by ▼. For this report, you will change the left and right margins and the first tab setting.

1. Move the cursor to the ruler:
   A. Open the Words menu.
   B. Select *Modify ruler*.
2. Set the left and right margins:
   A. Move the cursor to 1 inch by pressing → as needed.
   B. Set the left margin by pressing [.
   C. Move to 7 inches by pressing → as needed.
   D. Set the right margin by pressing].
3. Delete an unneeded tab setting:
   A. Move to the ▼ preceding 2 inches.
   B. Delete the unneeded tab setting by

pressing Delete.
4. Insert a tab setting at 2 inches:
   A. Move to 2 inches.
   B. Set a tab by pressing ! (an exclamation point).
5. Exit the ruler by pressing Ctrl-End.

CREATE A CALCULATED FIELD FOR SIDE-BY-SIDE FIELD DATA

The first line in the report heading includes the student's first and last names from the database file. To place the names side by side, you will create a calculated field to connect the two fields. Specifically, the calculated field will trim any blank spaces after each student's first name, insert one space after the first name, and then add the last name: TRIM(FNAME)+" "+LNAME.

1. With the cursor in the Detail Band, move to Line 6 by pressing ⏎ six times.
2. At the left margin, key **TO:**
3. Press Tab to move to Column 20.
4. Create a calculated field to insert the FNAME and LNAME data:
   A. Bring up a field list by pressing F5.
   B. Move to the CALCULATED column.
   C. Select <create>.
   D. Select *Expression* by pressing E.
   E. Key **TRIM(FNAME)+" "+LNAME** and press ⏎.
   F. Return to the Report Design screen by pressing Ctrl-End.
   G. Move to the end of the field by pressing End.

5. Key the remainder of the report heading:
    A. Move down two lines by pressing ↵ two times.
    B. Key **FROM:** and press Tab.
    C. Key **Patrick Sebrechts, Instructor** and then press ↵ two times.
    D. Key **DATE:** and press Tab.
    E. Key the current date and then press ↵ two times.
    F. Key **SUBJECT:** and press Tab.
    G. Key **Accounting Club Scholarship** and then press ↵ two times.

ENTER A PARAGRAPH INTO THE MAILMERGE REPORT

Next you will enter the first paragraph of the report.

1. Key the first paragraph of the report, as shown at the beginning of this application. Do not press ↵ anywhere within the paragraph.
2. At the end of the paragraph, press ↵ two times to leave a blank line between paragraphs.

ADD FIELDS

The second paragraph includes the GPA from the database file. As you key this paragraph, you will add the field from the database file.

1. Key the paragraph until the cursor is in position for the GPA.
2. Add the field from the database file:
    A. Bring up a field list by pressing F5.
    B. From the column of field names, select *GPA*.
    C. Select *Template* by pressing T.
    D. Change the template to **99.99** and press ↵.
    E. Return to the Report Design screen by pressing Ctrl-End.
    F. Move to the end of the field by pressing End.
3. Press the Spacebar and then key the remainder of the paragraph.

USE SPECIAL TEXT STYLES

To improve the report's appearance, you will change parts of the report heading to bold print (TO: FROM: DATE: SUBJECT:).

1. Use Arrows to move the cursor to **TO.**
2. Select **TO:**
    A. Begin the selection by pressing F6.
    B. Highlight **TO:** by pressing → two times.

C. Complete the selection by pressing ↵.
3. Change **TO:** to bold print:
    A. Open the Words menu.
    B. Select *Style.*
    C. Select *Bold.*
4. Repeat the preceding steps to change the remaining headings to bold (**FROM: DATE: SUBJECT:**).

VIEW THE REPORT ON THE SCREEN

To check the report format and content, you will view it on the screen.

1. Open the Print menu and select *View report on screen.*
2. Press the Spacebar to move through the report, noting the insertion of the name and GPA from the database file.
3. Return to the Report Design screen by pressing any key.

PRINT THE REPORT FROM THE REPORT DESIGN SCREEN

To prevent a blank page before each copy of the report, you will change the New Page selection and then print the report.

1. Open the Print menu.
2. Prevent blank pages during printing:
    A. Select *Control of printer.*
    B. Select *New page.*
    C. Change the selection to *NONE* by pressing the Spacebar.
    D. Close the submenu by pressing Esc.
3. Be sure your printer is ready.
4. Select *Begin printing.*

DESCRIBE AND SAVE THE REPORT FILE

1. Open the Layout menu and select *Edit description of report.*
2. Key **Scholarship report** and press ↵.
3. Open the Exit menu and select *Save changes and exit.*
4. Key **SCHOLAR** and press ↵.
5. To save the print form settings, select *Yes* and then accept the displayed filename by pressing ↵.

COMPLETE SUPPLEMENTARY APPLICATION 14

For additional practice with the procedures covered in this lesson, complete Supplementary Application 14 on page 103. Use the lesson summary on the following page as needed.

BEGIN A MAILMERGE REPORT FROM A QUICK LAYOUT 14A

Open a database file or a query file

From the Reports panel, select: *<create>*

From the Layout menu, select: *Quick layouts*

Select: *Mailmerge layout*

SET MARGINS AND TABS 14B

Open the Words menu

Select: *Modify ruler*

Move the cursor to the desired position

To set the left margin, press [

To set the right margin, press]

To clear a tab, press Delete

To set a tab, press ! (exclamation point)

Exit the ruler by pressing Ctrl-End

CREATE A CALCULATED FIELD FOR SIDE-BY-SIDE FIELD DATA 14C

Move the cursor into position for the field data

Bring up a field list by pressing F5

Move to the CALCULATED column

Select: *<create>*

Select: *Expression*

Enter an expression that will connect the fields, trim variable-length fields, and add spaces and punctuation as needed to separate the field data

Return to the Report Design screen by pressing Ctrl-End

Example: To place the first name and last name side by side, enter the following expression: **TRIM(FNAME)+″ ″+LNAME**.

ENTER A PARAGRAPH INTO THE MAILMERGE REPORT 14D

Key the paragraph like one long line; do not press ↵ within the paragraph

End the paragraph by pressing ↵ two times—once to end the paragraph and once to leave a blank line after the paragraph

ADD FIELDS 14E

Move the cursor into position for the field data

Bring up a field list by pressing F5

Select the field

Return to the Report Design screen by pressing Ctrl-End

USE SPECIAL TEXT STYLES 14F

Select the text:
  Move the cursor to the beginning of the text
  Press F6
  Highlight the text with →
  Complete the selection with ↵

Open the Words menu

Select: *Style*

Select the desired style

VIEW THE REPORT ON THE SCREEN 14G

Open the Print menu

Select: *View report on screen*

To continue the view, press the Spacebar

To cancel the view, press Esc

Return to the Report Design screen by pressing any key

PRINT THE REPORT FROM THE REPORT DESIGN SCREEN 14H

Open the Print menu

Prevent blank pages during printing:
  Select: *Control of printer*
  Select: *New page*
  Select: *NONE* (by pressing the Spacebar)
  Close the submenu by pressing Esc

Be sure your printer is ready

Select: *Begin printing*

DESCRIBE AND SAVE THE REPORT FILE 14I

Open the Layout menu

Select: *Edit description of report*

Enter the report description

Open the Exit menu

Select: *Save changes and exit*

Enter the report name

To save the print form settings, select: *Yes*; then accept the displayed filename by pressing ↵

• • • • • • • • • • • • • • •

LESSON 15: *MODIFYING THE FILE STRUCTURE AND ENTERING DATA INTO NEW FIELDS*

LESSON OBJECTIVES:

- Retrieve the database file structure
- Add new fields
- Save the modified file structure
- Delete a field
- Change a field characteristic
- Freeze a field
- Enter identical data into successive records
- Unfreeze a field
- Lock a field
- Unlock a field
- Save the changed file

APPLICATION 15: *MODIFYING THE FILE STRUCTURE AND ENTERING DATA INTO NEW FIELDS*

In this application, you will change the structure of the Primary file by adding, deleting, and changing fields. Then you will use special techniques to enter data for the new fields.

RETRIEVE THE DATABASE FILE STRUCTURE

To modify the structure of the Primary file, you will first retrieve the current file structure.

1. Open the Students catalog.
2. In the Data panel, highlight *PRIMARY* and press ↵.
3. Select *Modify structure/order*.
4. Close the Organize menu by pressing Esc.

ADD NEW FIELDS

You will add three fields to the Primary file: PHONE, ADVISOR, and BIRTHDATE.

1. Add PHONE as Field 5:
   A. Move to Field 5 (the GPA field) by pressing ↓ as needed.
   B. Insert a blank line by pressing Ctrl-N.
   C. Key **PHONE** and press ↵.
   D. Accept *Character* by pressing ↵.
   E. Key **14** and press ↵.
   F. Accept *No index* by pressing ↵.
2. Add ADVISOR as Field 8 and BIRTHDATE as Field 9:
   A. Move to Field 8 by pressing ↓ two times.
   B. Add ADVISOR, a character field, 20 spaces wide, no index.
   C. At Field 9, add BIRTHDATE, a date field, no index.

SAVE THE MODIFIED FILE STRUCTURE

You can make almost any change in the database file structure without losing your data. Certain kinds of changes, however, should not be made at the same time. For example, do not change a field name and its width at the same time. As a safeguard, you will save the modified file structure after each type of change.

1. Open the Exit menu and select *Save changes and exit*.
2. When asked if you are sure you want to save the changes, select *Yes*.

DELETE A FIELD

When you delete a field from the file structure, the data for that field is erased from all records. This is a serious change that cannot be undone. You will delete the ENRDATE field.

1. Retrieve the database file structure.
2. Move to the ENRDATE field.
3. Delete the field by pressing Ctrl-U.
4. Save the modified file structure.

CHANGE A FIELD CHARACTERISTIC

You can change any of the field characteristics. However, as a safeguard, you should save the file structure after you change each characteristic. You will change the width of the FNAME field.

1. Retrieve the database file structure.
2. Move to the FNAME field.
3. Tab to the Width column.
4. Erase the current width by pressing Ctrl-Y or Delete.
5. Key **8** and press ↵.
6. Save the modified file structure.

FREEZE A FIELD

You are now ready to enter the data for the PHONE field. To save time, you will freeze the field so that the cursor will stay in the field from record to record.

1. With *PRIMARY* highlighted in the Data panel, display the records by pressing F2. If all records are not displayed, press PgUp.
2. Freeze the PHONE field:
   A. Open the Fields menu.
   B. Select *Freeze field*.
   C. Key **PHONE** and press ↵.
3. Enter the telephone numbers as shown; do not press ↵:
   A. For Patt Sharp, **(314) 888-7823**
   B. For Bill Sharp, **(314) 889-4577**
   C. For Liu, **(619) 445-3322**
   D. For Cruse, **(619) 882-4489**
   E. For Roodman, **(314) 443-2245**
4. When asked if you want to *Add new records?* select *No*.

ENTER IDENTICAL DATA INTO SUCCESSIVE RECORDS

The first three students have the same advisor (Haugland) and the last two students have the same advisor (Beard). You will freeze the ADVISOR field and then use Shift-F8, the ditto key, to enter the duplicate advisor names.

1. Freeze the ADVISOR field:
   A. Open the Fields menu.
   B. Select *Freeze field*.
   C. Erase *PHONE* by pressing Backspace as needed.
   D. Key **ADVISOR** and press ↵.
2. Enter the advisors as follows:
   A. Move to the top record by pressing PgUp.
   B. For Patt Sharp, key **Haugland** and press ↵.
   C. For Bill Sharp, repeat Haugland by pressing Shift-F8 and then ↵.
   D. For Liu, repeat Haugland by pressing Shift-F8 and then ↵.
   E. For Cruse, key **Beard** and press ↵.
   F. For Roodman, repeat Beard by pressing Shift-F8 and then ↵.
3. When asked if you want to *Add new records?*, select *No*.

UNFREEZE A FIELD

In preparation for locking a field in the following section, you will now unfreeze the ADVISOR field.

1. Open the Fields menu.
2. Select *Freeze field*.
3. Erase **ADVISOR** by pressing Backspace as needed.
4. Press ↵.

LOCK A FIELD

The SS_NO field is no longer showing at the left of the screen. You will need these numbers to identify the students when you enter their birthdates. Therefore, you will lock the SS_NO field on the screen.

1. Display the SS_NO field at the left of the screen by pressing Home.
2. Tab to the LNAME field (the field to the right of the field to be frozen).
3. Lock the SS_NO field on the screen:
   A. Open the Fields menu.

B. Select *Lock fields on left*.
C. Key **1** (do not press ↵).
4. Freeze the BIRTHDATE field:
   A. Open the Fields menu.
   B. Select *Freeze field*.
   C. Key **BIRTHDATE** and press ↵.
5. The locked SS_NO field is displayed at the right and the cursor is in the frozen BIRTHDATE field. Move to the top record by pressing PgUp.
6. Enter the following birthdates—do not press ↵:
   A. For 236-44-9987, key **082457**
   B. For 287-88-3478, key **100641**
   C. For 423-32-6777, key **011143**
   D. For 432-22-6789, key **110242**
   E. For 924-33-4689, key **032041**
7. When asked if you want to *Add new records?*, select *No*.

UNLOCK A FIELD

Now that you are finished with the data entry, you will unlock the SS_NO field.

1. Open the Fields menu.
2. Select *Lock fields on left*.
3. Key **0** (the number 0).

When you exit the Browse screen, dBASE IV automatically unlocks and unfreezes fields. You unlocked the SS_NO field just for practice.

SAVE THE CHANGED FILE

1. Open the Exit menu.
2. Select *Exit*.

COMPLETE SUPPLEMENTARY APPLICATION 15

For additional practice with the procedures covered in this lesson, complete Supplementary Application 15 on page 104. Use the lesson summary on the following page as needed.

RETRIEVE THE DATABASE FILE STRUCTURE   15A

In the Data panel, highlight the database filename

Press ↵

Select: *Modify structure/order*

Close the Organize menu by pressing Esc

ADD NEW FIELDS   15B

If the field is to be inserted between existing fields, open a blank line by pressing Ctrl-N

OR if the field is to be inserted at the end, press ↓ to move to the end of the list

Enter the field as usual

SAVE THE MODIFIED FILE STRUCTURE   15C

Open the Exit menu

Select: *Save changes and exit*

Select: *Yes*

DELETE A FIELD   15D

Retrieve the database file structure

Move the cursor to the field

Press Ctrl-U

Save the modified file structure

CHANGE A FIELD CHARACTERISTIC   15E

Retrieve the database file structure

Move to the characteristic to be changed:
   To move forward, press Tab
   To move backward, press Shift-Tab

Make the desired change

If the cursor remains in the column, press ↵ to complete the change

Save the modified file structure

FREEZE A FIELD   15F

Display the database records

On the Browse screen, open the Fields menu

Select: *Freeze field*

Enter the name of the field to be frozen

ENTER IDENTICAL DATA INTO SUCCESSIVE RECORDS   15G

With the cursor in the field, press Shift-F8

UNFREEZE A FIELD   15H

On the Browse screen, open the Fields menu

Select: *Freeze field*

Erase the field name by pressing Backspace as needed

Press ↵

LOCK A FIELD   15I

At the left side of the Browse screen, display the field that is to be locked

Move the highlighting to the right of the field to be locked

Open the Fields menu

Select: *Lock fields on left*

Key the number of fields to be locked

UNLOCK A FIELD   15J

On the Browse screen, open the Fields menu

Select: *Lock fields on left*

Enter **0**

SAVE THE CHANGED FILE   15K

Open the Exit menu

Select: *Exit*

LESSON 16: *CREATING AND USING LINKED DATABASE FILES*

LESSON OBJECTIVES:

- Create a file to be linked
- Select the files to be linked
- Link the files
- Describe and save the linked view
- Modify a query
- Select fields for a linked view
- Select records for a linked view
- Select an index for a linked view
- Save the modified query

APPLICATION 16: *CREATING AND USING LINKED DATABASE FILES*

In this application, you will create a new database file for student addresses. Then you will link the Primary and Address files so that you can retrieve information from both files at the same time.

CREATE A FILE TO BE LINKED

You will create an Address database file for the students. So that you can later link this file to the Primary file, you will include a common field—the SS_NO field.

1. Open the Students catalog.
2. From the Data panel, select <create>.
3. Referring to Lesson 1 as needed, define the file structure:

Name	Field Type	Width	Dec	Index
SS_NO	Character	11		Y
STREET	Character	20		N
CITY	Character	15		N
STATE	Character	2		N
ZIP	Character	5		N

4. Save the file structure by opening the Exit menu and selecting *Save changes and exit*. Enter **ADDRESS** as the filename.
5. With *ADDRESS* highlighted in the Data panel, bring up the Edit screen by pressing F2.
6. Referring to Lesson 2 as needed, enter the following records into the Address file:

   236-44-9987
   820 Themis
   Cape Girardeau
   MO
   63701

   287-88-3478
   987 College
   Kennett
   MO
   63854

   423-32-6777
   35 Barnard
   Oceanside
   CA
   92007

   432-22-6789
   1019 Valencia
   San Marcos
   CA
   92069

   924-33-4689
   7894 Kingway
   Sikeston
   MO
   63801

7. Save the records by opening the Exit menu and selecting *Exit*.

SELECT THE FILES TO BE LINKED

To select the Primary and Address files as the files to be linked, you will include both files in a query.

1. Open the Primary file (highlight, ↵, select *Use file*).
2. From the Queries panel, select <create>.
3. Include the Primary file indexes:
   A. Open the Fields menu.
   B. Select *Include indexes*.
4. Add the Address file and its indexes to the query:
   A. Open the Layout menu.
   B. Select *Add file to query*.
   C. Select *ADDRESS.DBF*.
   D. Open the Fields menu.
   E. Select *Include indexes*.

LINK THE FILES

You will link the Primary and Address files by identifying the common field—the SS_NO field.

1. Move up to the Primary file skeleton by pressing F3.
2. Tab to the SS_NO field.
3. Open the Layout menu.
4. Select *Create link by pointing*. **LINK1** will be displayed in the field.
5. Move down to the Address file skeleton by pressing F4.
6. Tab to the SS_NO field.
7. Complete the link by pressing ↵.

DESCRIBE AND SAVE THE LINKED VIEW

You will now save the linked view on your data disk so that you can use the view each time you need information from both files at the same time. The linked view (a query file) will not replace the individual database files on your disk. The view will simply provide a link between the files.

1. Open the Layout menu and select *Edit description of query*.
2. Key **Primary and Address files** and press ↵.
3. Open the Exit menu and select *Save changes and exit*.
4. Key **LINKED** and press ↵.

MODIFY A QUERY

For practice in selecting fields, records, and an index for a linked view, you will modify the Linked query.

1. With *LINKED* highlighted in the Queries panel, press ↵.
2. Select *Modify query*.

SELECT FIELDS FOR A LINKED VIEW

You will select the following fields for the view: FNAME, LNAME, STREET, CITY, STATE, ZIP.

1. Clear all fields from the view skeleton:
   A. Move up to the Primary file skeleton by pressing F3.
   B. Move to the filename (*Primary.dbf*) by pressing Home.
   C. Clear all fields from the view skeleton by pressing F5 (for Releases 1.5 and 2.0, press F5 a second time).
2. From the Primary file, select FNAME and then LNAME for the view:
   A. Tab to the FNAME field; then press F5 to select the field.
   B. Move to the LNAME field by pressing Shift-Tab; then press F5 to select the field.
3. From the Address file, select STREET, CITY, STATE, and ZIP:
   A. Move down to the Address file skeleton by pressing F4.
   B. Tab to the STREET field; press F5.
   C. Tab to the CITY field; press F5.
   D. Tab to the STATE field; press F5.
   E. Tab to the ZIP field; press F5.

SELECT RECORDS FOR A LINKED VIEW

You will select the records of all non-transfer students who are from Missouri.

1. Move up to the Primary file skeleton by pressing F3.
2. Move to the TRANSFER field.
3. For the search condition, key **.F.** and press ↵.
4. Move down to the Address file skeleton by pressing F4.
5. Move to the STATE field.
6. Key **"MO"** (including uppercase and the quotation marks) and press ↵.

SELECT AN INDEX FOR A LINKED VIEW

For this query, you will select the Name index from the Primary file.

1. Move up to the Primary file skeleton by pressing F3.
2. Tab to the LNAME+FNAME index column (listed after the field names).
3. Open the Fields menu.
4. Select *Sort on this field*.
5. Select *Ascending ASCII*.
6. Apply the query by pressing F2. Two records will be displayed: Toby Roodman and Bill Sharp.
7. Return to the Query Design screen by opening the Exit menu and selecting *Transfer to query design*.

SAVE THE MODIFIED QUERY

1. Open the Exit menu.
2. Select *Save changes and exit*.

COMPLETE SUPPLEMENTARY APPLICATION 16

For additional practice with the procedures covered in this lesson, complete Supplementary Application 16 on page 105. Use the lesson summary on the following page as needed.

SUMMARY: CREATING AND USING LINKED DATABASE FILES

CREATE A FILE TO BE LINKED   16A

Create the second database file as usual, including a common field (a field that is the same in both files)

SELECT THE FILES TO BE LINKED   16B

Open the most important database file:
    In the Data panel, highlight the database filename
    Press ↵
    Select: *Use file*

From the Queries panel, select: *<create>*

Open the Fields menu

Select: *Include indexes*

Open the Layout menu

Select: *Add file to query*

From the displayed list of files, select the next database file

Open the Fields menu

Select: *Include indexes*

(If additional files are to be linked, open the Layout menu, add the file, and include the indexes. Up to eight files can be linked in the query.)

LINK THE FILES   16C

Move back to the file skeleton of the first file by pressing F3

Move to the common field

Open the Layout menu

Select: *Create link by pointing*

Move to the file skeleton of the second file by pressing F4

Move to the common field in the second file

Complete the link by pressing ↵

DESCRIBE AND SAVE THE LINKED VIEW   16D

Open the Layout menu

Select: *Edit description of query*

Enter the description of the view

Open the Exit menu

Select: *Save changes and exit*

Enter the query name

MODIFY A QUERY   16E

In the Queries panel, highlight the query name

Press ↵

Select: *Modify query*

Select fields, select records, and/or select an index, as outlined

SELECT FIELDS FOR A LINKED VIEW   16F

In the first file skeleton, move to the database filename

Clear all fields from the view by pressing F5 (for Releases 1.5 and 2.0, press F5 a second time)

Select fields for the view:

    Move to the desired file skeleton by pressing F4 (forward) or F3 (backward)
    Move to the desired field by pressing Tab (forward) or Shift-Tab (backward)
    Select the field by pressing F5

SELECT RECORDS FOR A LINKED VIEW   16G

Move to the file skeleton containing the condition field by pressing F3 or F4

Move to the condition field

Enter the condition(s)

SELECT AN INDEX FOR A LINKED VIEW   16H

Move to the file skeleton containing the index field

Move to the index field

Open the Fields menu

Select: *Sort on this field*

Select the type of sort

SAVE THE MODIFIED QUERY   16I

Open the Exit menu

Select: *Save changes and exit*

LESSON 17: *CREATING LABELS*

LESSON OBJECTIVES:

- Begin a label file
- Change the label selection
- Change the left margin of the labels
- Create a calculated field to insert side-by-side field data
- Add a field
- View the labels on the screen
- Describe and save the label file

APPLICATION 17: CREATING LABELS

In this application, you will create the following labels for the non-transfer students from Missouri.

```
Toby Roodman                    Bill Sharp
7894 Kingway                    987 College
Sikeston, MO    63801           Kennett, MO    63854
```

BEGIN A LABEL FILE

The labels include the first and last names from the Primary file and the addresses from the Address file. Therefore, you will open the Linked query you created in the preceding lesson and then begin the label file.

1. Open the Linked query:
   A. Open the Students catalog.
   B. In the Queries panel, highlight *LINKED* and press ↵.
   C. Select *Use view*.
2. From the Labels panel, select *<create>*.

CHANGE THE LABEL SELECTION

The current label selection is a single row of labels, 15/16" deep x 3 1/2" wide (15/16 x 3 1/2 x 1). You will change the selection to a double row of side-by-side labels, the same size (15/16 x 3 1/2 x 2).

1. Open the Dimensions menu.
2. Select *Predefined Size*.
3. Select *15/16 x 3 1/2 x 2*.

You will not see the double row of labels on the Label Design screen, but you will see the double row when you view the labels later.

CHANGE THE LEFT MARGIN OF THE LABELS

As shown in the ruler at the top of the label, the left margin is currently at 0 inches. You will change the left margin so that the printing will begin a half inch from the left edge of the label.

1. Open the Words menu.
2. Select *Modify ruler*.
3. Move the cursor to a half inch by pressing → five times.
4. Set a new left margin by pressing [.
5. Exit the ruler by pressing Ctrl-End.
6. Move down to Line 1 and the new left margin by pressing ↵.

CREATE A CALCULATED FIELD TO INSERT SIDE-BY-SIDE FIELD DATA

The first line of the label includes the student's first name and last name, side by side. To connect the data appropriately, you will create a calculated field. Specifically, this field will trim the FNAME data (removing any blank spaces at the end of the name), insert one blank space between names, and then insert the LNAME data.

1. At the beginning of Line 1, bring up a field list by pressing F5.
2. Move to the CALCULATED column by pressing →.
3. Select *<create>*.
4. On the submenu, select *Expression* by pressing E.
5. Key **TRIM(FNAME)+" "+LNAME** and press ↵.
6. No other selections are necessary; return to the Label Design screen by pressing Ctrl-End.

ADD A FIELD

Next you will add the STREET field on the second line of the label.

1. Move to the next line of the label by pressing ↵.
2. Bring up a field list by pressing F5.
3. From the LINKED column, select *STREET*.
4. Return to the Label Design screen by pressing Ctrl-End.

CREATE A SECOND CALCULATED FIELD TO INSERT SIDE-BY-SIDE FIELD DATA

The last line of the label includes the city, state, and ZIP. You will create a calculated field to connect these fields appropriately. Specifically, this field will trim the CITY data, insert a comma and one blank space after the city, insert the STATE data, insert two blank spaces after the state, and then insert the ZIP data.

1. Move to the next line of the label by pressing ↵.
2. Bring up a field list by pressing F5.
3. Move to the CALCULATED column by pressing →.
4. Select *<create>*.
5. Select *Expression* by pressing E.
6. Key **TRIM(CITY)+", "+STATE+" "+ZIP** and press ↵.
7. Return to the Label Design screen by pressing Ctrl-End.

VIEW THE LABELS ON THE SCREEN

Before saving the file, you will check the labels on the screen.

1. Open the Print menu.
2. Select *View labels on screen*. The labels for Toby Roodman and Bill Sharp (the Missouri, non-transfer students) are displayed.
3. Return to the Label Design screen by pressing Esc and then any key.

DESCRIBE AND SAVE THE LABEL FILE

1. Open the Layout menu and select *Edit description of label design*.
2. Key **Non-transfer Missouri students** and press ↵.
3. Open the Exit menu and select *Save changes and exit*.
4. Key **NON_TRAN** and press ↵.

COMPLETE SUPPLEMENTARY APPLICATION 17

For additional practice with the procedures covered in this lesson, complete Supplementary Application 17 on page 106. Use the lesson summary on the following page as needed.

SUMMARY: CREATING LABELS

BEGIN A LABEL FILE 17A

Open a database file or a query file

From the Labels panel, select: *<create>*

CHANGE THE LABEL SELECTION 17B

Open the Dimensions menu

Select: *Predefined size*

Select a size from those listed, OR press Esc and change any of the listed options

CHANGE THE LEFT MARGIN OF THE LABELS 17C

Open the Words menu

Select: *Modify ruler*

Move the cursor to the desired left margin

Set a new left margin by pressing [

Exit the ruler by pressing Ctrl-End

CREATE A CALCULATED FIELD TO INSERT SIDE-BY-SIDE FIELD DATA 17D

Move the cursor into position for the field data

Bring up a field list by pressing F5

Move to the CALCULATED column

Select: *<create>*

Select: *Expression*

Enter an expression that will connect the fields, trim variable-length data, and add spaces and punctuation as needed to separate the data

Return to the Report Design screen by pressing Ctrl-End

Example: To place the city, state, and ZIP on a line side by side, enter the following expression: **TRIM(CITY)+", "+STATE+" "+ZIP**

ADD A FIELD 17E

Move the cursor into position for the field data

Bring up a field list by pressing F5

Select the field

Return to the Report Design screen by pressing Ctrl-End

VIEW THE LABELS ON THE SCREEN 17F

Open the Print menu

Select: *View labels on screen*

To continue the view, press the Spacebar

To cancel the view, press Esc

Return to the Label Design screen by pressing any key

DESCRIBE AND SAVE THE LABEL FILE 17G

Open the Layout menu

Select: *Edit description of label design*

Enter the description

Open the Exit menu

Select: *Save changes and exit*

Enter the labels name

LESSON 18: *WORKING WITH MEMO FIELDS*

LESSON OBJECTIVES:

- Define a memo field in the file structure
- Enter data into a memo field
- Create a report including a memo field
- Edit a memo field

APPLICATION 18: *WORKING WITH MEMO FIELDS*

In this application, you will add a memo field to the Primary file. Then you will enter memo field data for two students, create a report that includes the memo field, and finally edit a memo field.

DEFINE A MEMO FIELD IN THE FILE STRUCTURE

*A memo field is a field in which you can store large blocks of data in free-form style (arranged however you want it). You can store as many as 64,000 characters in the memo field of each record. You will modify the Primary file structure by adding a memo field named **ACTIVITIES** as Field 7.*

1. Open the Students catalog.
2. In the Data panel, highlight *PRIMARY* and press ⏎.
3. Select *Modify structure/order*.
4. Close the Organize menu by pressing Esc.
5. Move to Field 7 (ADVISOR) by pressing ↓ as needed.
6. Open a blank line by pressing Ctrl-N.
7. For the field name, key **ACTIVITIES** but do not press ⏎ because the field name will fill the column and the cursor will jump to the field type.
8. In the field type column, press the Spacebar until *Memo* is displayed; then press ⏎. The cursor moves down to the next field because a memo field is automatically assigned a width of 10 spaces in the file structure, does not have a set number of decimal places, and cannot be indexed.
9. Save the modified file structure:
   A. Open the Exit menu.
   B. Select *Save changes and exit*.
   C. When asked if you are sure you want to save the changes, select *Yes*.

ENTER DATA INTO A MEMO FIELD

You will use the memo field to record the activities of two students.

1. With *PRIMARY* highlighted in the Data panel, bring up the records by pressing F2.
2. On either the Browse screen or the Edit screen, move to the Patt Sharp record (the top record).
3. Move to the ACTIVITIES field.
4. With the cursor in the memo field, zoom to the memo screen by pressing F9.

5. On the open screen, key the following activities. Do not press ⏎ until you have keyed an entire paragraph (block of text); then press ⏎ two times, as shown:
   STUDENT ORGANIZATIONS: Student Council, Varsity Cheerleaders, Kappa Delta Pi, Baptist Student Union, Accounting Club⏎
   ⏎
   CAMPUS EMPLOYMENT: Library assistant, instructor aide for the English Department, concessions attendant⏎
   ⏎
6. Save the memo data:
   A. Open the Exit menu.
   B. Select *Save changes and exit*.

*dBASE IV changes **memo** to **MEMO** after data has been entered in the memo field.*

7. Move to the Liu record.
8. In the ACTIVITIES field, zoom to the memo screen by pressing F9.
9. Key the following activities:
   STUDENT ORGANIZATIONS: Society for the Advancement of Management, Marketing Club, Young Republicans⏎
   ⏎
   CAMPUS EMPLOYMENT: Bookstore clerk⏎
   ⏎
10. To save the memo data, use a shortcut: Press F9.
11. Save the changed file:
    A. Open the Exit menu.
    B. Select *Exit*.

CREATE A REPORT INCLUDING A MEMO FIELD

You will create a column report that includes the FNAME, LNAME, and ACTIVITIES fields from the Primary file.

1. With the Primary file open, select *<create>* from the Reports panel.
2. Close the Layout menu by pressing Esc.
3. Change the report margins:
   A. Open the Words menu.
   B. Select *Modify ruler*.

C. Move the cursor to 1 inch by pressing → as needed.

D. Set the left margin by pressing [.

E. Move the cursor to 7 inches by pressing → as needed.

F. Set the right margin by pressing].

G. Exit the ruler by pressing Ctrl-End.

4. Enter a report title:

A. Move into the Page Header Band by pressing ↓.

B. Move the cursor to Line 6, Column 30 (as shown in the status bar) by pressing ↵ and → as needed.

C. Key **STUDENT ACTIVITIES REPORT**.

5. Add the report fields (FNAME, LNAME, and ACTIVITIES) to the Detail Band:

A. Move into the Detail Band.

B. Move to Column 10 by pressing → as needed.

C. Bring up a field list by pressing F5.

D. Highlight *FNAME* and press ↵.

E. Press Ctrl-End.

F. Move to Column 20.

G. Bring up a field list by pressing F5.

H. Highlight *LNAME* and press ↵.

I. Press Ctrl-End.

J. Move to Column 40.

K. Bring up a field list by pressing F5.

L. With *ACTIVITIES* highlighted, press ↵.

M. Press Ctrl-End.

6. The memo size (the Vs in the Detail Band) currently extends to 9 inches—beyond the right margin. Decrease the memo field size to end at the right margin:

A. Move to the beginning of the memo field data (Column 40).

B. Begin the resizing by pressing Shift-F7.

C. Press ← until the cursor is in Column 70 (at the right margin).

D. Complete the resizing by pressing ↵.

7. Insert a blank line between the records:

A. Move the cursor to the end of the Detail Band by pressing End.

B. Insert a blank line by pressing ↵.

8. View the report on the screen:

A. Open the Print menu.

B. Select *View report on screen*.

C. Return to the Report Design screen by pressing any key.

9. Describe and save the report file:

A. Open the Layout menu and select *Edit description of report*.

B. Key **Student activities** and press ↵.

C. Open the Exit menu and select *Save changes and exit*.

D. Key **ACTIVITY** and press ↵.

EDIT A MEMO FIELD

You can edit a memo field from either the Edit screen or the Browse screen. You will add an additional student organization to the Liu record.

1. In the Data panel, highlight *PRIMARY*.

2. Bring up the records by pressing F2.

3. On the Edit or Browse screen, move to the Liu record.

4. Move to the *ACTIVITIES* field.

5. With the cursor in the memo field, press F9.

6. Use Arrow keys to move the cursor to the end of the STUDENT ORGANIZATION paragraph.

7. Add **Editorial Board** to the list of activities.

8. Save the edited memo data by again pressing F9.

9. Return to the Control Center:

A. Open the Exit menu.

B. Select *Exit*.

COMPLETE SUPPLEMENTARY APPLICATION 18

For additional practice with the procedures covered in this lesson, complete Supplementary Application 18 on page 107. Use the lesson summary on the following page as needed.

DEFINE A MEMO FIELD IN THE FILE STRUCTURE 18A

Enter the field name

In the field type column, press the Spacebar until Memo is displayed; then press ↵

The cursor will move to the next field because a memo field is automatically assigned a width of 10 in the file structure, has no set number of decimal places, and cannot be indexed

ENTER DATA INTO A MEMO FIELD 18B

On the Edit or Browse screen, move to the Memo field

Zoom to an open screen by pressing F9

Key the data on the screen

Save the memo data:
Open the Exit menu
Select: *Save changes and exit*

Shortcut: Save the memo data by pressing F9 again.

CREATE A REPORT INCLUDING A MEMO FIELD 18C

Open a database file or a query file that includes the memo field

From the Reports panel, select: *<create>*

From the Layout menu, select: *Quick layouts.*

Select: *Column layout* or *Form layout* or *Mailmerge layout* (OR close the Layout menu by pressing Esc and create the report from scratch)

Change the report margins as needed

In the Page Header Band, insert a report title and column headings if needed

In the Detail Band, add the fields from the database file, including the memo field:
Bring up a field list by pressing F5
Select the field
Press Ctrl-End

Size the memo field:
In the Detail Band, move to the beginning of the memo data
Press Shift-F7
Press ← until the memo data fits the margins
Complete the sizing by pressing ↵

Prevent blank pages during printing:
Open the Print menu
Select: *Control of printer*
Select: *New page*
Select: *NONE*
Close the submenu by pressing Esc

View the report on the screen:
From the Print menu, select: *View report on screen*
Move through the report by pressing the Spacebar
Return to the Report Design screen by pressing any key

Describe and save the report file:
Open the Layout menu
Select: *Edit description of* report
Enter the description
Open the Exit menu
Select: *Save changes and exit*
Enter the report name

EDIT A MEMO FIELD 18D

On the Edit or Browse screen, move to the record to be changed

Move to the memo field

Zoom to the current memo data by pressing F9

Make the desired changes

Save the changed memo data by again pressing F9

Save the changed file:
Open the Exit menu
Select: *Exit*

LESSON 19: *CREATING A FORM FOR DATA ENTRY OR EDITING*

LESSON OBJECTIVES:

- Begin a form file from scratch
- Draw a box
- Add the needed fields
- Prevent a field from being edited
- Save the form
- Use the form to edit the file
- Display the original Edit or Browse screen

APPLICATION 19: CREATING A FORM FOR DATA ENTRY OR EDITING

In this application, you will create and use the following form to change the GPA's of the students in the Primary file.

```
┌─────────────────────────────────────────────┐
│           FORM FOR CHANGING GPA              │
└─────────────────────────────────────────────┘

SOCIAL SECURITY NUMBER:   XXXXXXXXXXX    GPA:   99.99
```

In previous lessons, you edited the records on the Edit and Browse screens. As you recall, each of these screens lists all of the database fields in the order they appear in the file structure.

In addition to the Edit and Browse screens, you can design special editing screens—called forms—that include only the fields you need for specific editing.

BEGIN A FORM FILE FROM SCRATCH

First, you will open the Primary file and begin a form file from scratch.

1. Open the Students catalog.
2. Open the Primary file.
3. From the Forms panel, select *<create>*.

DRAW A BOX

For emphasis, the title of the form can be placed inside a box. You will draw a box and then key the title.

1. Open the Layout menu.
2. Select *Box*.
3. Select *Single line*.
4. Move to the upper-left corner of the box by pressing Arrow keys as needed (Row 2, Column 13, as shown in the status bar).
5. Select this position as the upper-left corner of the box by pressing ↵.
6. Extend the box by pressing ↓ two times and then → as needed to move to Column 55.
7. Complete the box by pressing ↵.
8. Use Arrow keys to move into the box (Row 3, Column 24) and key **FORM FOR CHANGING GPA**.

ADD THE NEEDED FIELDS

For GPA changes, the only fields you need are the SS_NO and GPA fields. (The SS_NO field is needed to identify the students.) You will add these fields side by side, as shown at the top of this application.

1. Move to Row 7, Column 10 by pressing Arrow keys as needed.
2. Key **SOCIAL SECURITY NUMBER:**
3. Move to Column 35 by pressing → two times.
4. Add the SS_NO field data:
   A. Bring up a field list by pressing F5.
   B. Select *SS_NO*.
   C. Press Ctrl-End.
5. Move to Column 50 by pressing → as needed.
6. Key **GPA:**
7. Move to Column 56 by pressing → two times.
8. Add the GPA field data:
   A. Bring up a field list by pressing F5.
   B. Select *GPA*.
   C. Press Ctrl-End.

PREVENT A FIELD FROM BEING EDITED

You designed this form to use when you edit the GPA field. During this editing, you do not want to permit any changes in the Social Security numbers. Therefore, you will prevent any editing in the SS_NO field.

1. Move to Column 35, the beginning of the SS_NO field data.
2. Open the Fields menu.
3. Select *Modify field*.
4. Select *Edit options*.

5. Change the highlighted *Editing allowed YES* to *NO* by pressing the Spacebar.
6. Accept the change by pressing Ctrl-End two times.

SAVE THE FORM

Now that the form is complete, you will save it on your data disk.

1. Open the Exit menu.
2. Select *Save changes and exit*.
3. For the form name, key **GPA** and press ↵.

USE THE FORM TO EDIT THE FILE

You will now use the form to update each student's GPA.

1. Bring up the form:
   A. With GPA highlighted in the Forms panel, press ↵.
   B. Select *Display data*.
2. If Record 1 is not displayed (as shown in the status bar), press PgUp as needed to move to Record 1.
3. Change the GPA of each student by keying the new GPA shown below; do not press ↵ because the number will fill the field.

If you plan to use the numeric keypad to enter the data, be sure Num Lock is on.

SS_NO	GPA
236-44-9987	**3.45**
287-88-3478	**3.84**
423-32-6777	**3.39**
432-22-6789	**3.97**
924-33-4689	**3.84**

4. When asked if you want to *Add new records?*, select *No*.
5. Save the edited file:
   A. Open the Exit menu.
   B. Select *Exit*.

DISPLAY THE ORIGINAL EDIT OR BROWSE SCREEN

After you have used a form to edit the file, you will often need to return to the original Edit or Browse screen to perform other database activities. To exit the form, you will close the Primary file and then reopen it.

1. Close the Primary file:
   A. With *PRIMARY* highlighted in the Data panel, press ↵.
   B. Select *Close file*.
2. Re-open the Primary file:
   A. In the Data panel, highlight *PRIMARY* and press ↵.
   B. Select *Use file*.
3. Display the original Edit screen by pressing F2.
4. Switch to the original Browse screen by pressing F2 again.
5. Return to the Control Center by opening the Exit menu and selecting *Exit*.

COMPLETE SUPPLEMENTARY APPLICATION 19

For additional practice with the procedures covered in this lesson, complete Supplementary Application 19 on page 108. Use the lesson summary on the following page as needed.

BEGIN A FORM FILE FROM SCRATCH · 19A

Open a database file

From the Forms panel, select: *<create>*

Close the Layout menu by pressing Esc

DRAW A BOX · 19B

Open the Layout menu

Select: *Box*

Select: *Single line*

Use Arrows to move the cursor to the upper-left corner of the box

Press ↵

Use Arrows to extend the box down and to the right

Complete the box by pressing ↵

ADD THE NEEDED FIELDS · 19C

Move the cursor into position for the field heading

Key the field heading

Move the cursor into position for the field data

Add the field data:
Bring up a field list by pressing F5
Select the field
Press Ctrl-End

PREVENT A FIELD FROM BEING EDITED · 19D

On the Form Design screen, move to the field data that is not to be edited

Open the Fields menu

Select: *Modify field*

Select: *Edit options*

Change *Editing allowed YES* to *NO* by pressing ↵

Save the changes by pressing Ctrl-End two times

SAVE THE FORM · 19E

Open the Exit menu

Select: *Save changes and exit*

Enter the form name

USE THE FORM TO EDIT THE FILE · 19F

In the Forms panel, highlight the form name

Press ↵

Select: *Display data*

Make the desired changes

Save the edited file:
Open the Exit menu
Select: *Exit*

DISPLAY THE ORIGINAL EDIT OR BROWSE SCREEN · 19G

Close the open database file:
In the Data panel, highlight the database file-name
Press ↵
Select: *Close file*

Re-open the database file:
In the Data panel, highlight the database file-name
Press ↵
Select: *Use file*

Display the records by pressing F2

Return to the Control Center:
Open the Exit menu
Select: *Exit*

LESSON 20: *GETTING HELP WITH dBASE IV*

LESSON OBJECTIVES:

- Bring up a Help screen
- Review the Help information
- Use the Contents option
- Use the Related Topics option
- Back up to the preceding Help screen
- Print a Help screen
- Exit Help
- Get help with a specific screen
- Get help with file management

APPLICATION 20: GETTING HELP WITH dBASE IV

In this application, you will use the dBASE IV Help feature to review several of the procedures you have learned and to preview some new procedures. The Help feature will be very important as you continue to use and learn dBASE IV.

BRING UP A HELP SCREEN

When you press F1, dBASE IV provides on-screen help for the current screen or for a highlighted menu option. You will bring up the Help screen for the <create> option in the Data panel.

1. In the Data panel, highlight <create>.
2. Bring up the Help screen by pressing F1.

REVIEW THE HELP INFORMATION

*The Help screen displays information on the topic listed at the top of the screen. When **<MORE F4>** is displayed at the lower right of the Help screen, you can get more help on the topic by pressing F4. You will review the Help information for creating a database file.*

1. Read the first Help screen that is displayed.
2. When you see <MORE F4>, bring up the next Help screen by pressing F4.
3. When <MORE F4> no longer appears, you are at the end of the Help information on the current topic.

At this point, you could exit Help by pressing Esc. Instead, in the next several sections of this application, you will learn to use the Help menu bar at the bottom of the Help screen.

USE THE CONTENTS OPTION

The Help menu bar includes a CONTENTS option. This option provides a list of additional topics concerning database files. To see this list, you will select CONTENTS from the Help menu bar. Then you will review one of the additional topics.

1. With *CONTENTS* highlighted in the Help menu bar, select the option by pressing **C** or ↵.
2. From the contents list, select *About Database Files*.
3. Read the Help screen for this topic.

USE THE RELATED TOPICS OPTION

dBASE IV also provides a list of topics related to the current Help topic. To see this list, you will select RELATED TOPICS from the Help menu bar. Then you will review one of the related topics.

1. From the Help menu bar, select *RELATED TOPICS* by pressing **R** (or → and ↵).
2. From the list, select *Navigating the Database Design Screen* by pressing ↓ and ↵.
3. Read the Help screen for this topic.

BACK UP TO THE PRECEDING HELP SCREEN

You can review the preceding Help screens by selecting BACKUP from the Help menu bar or by pressing F3. You will practice each of these procedures.

1. First, back up to the preceding Help screen by selecting *BACKUP* from the Help menu bar.
2. Next, back up several screens by pressing F3 repeatedly.

PRINT A HELP SCREEN

The PRINT option on the Help menu bar enables you to print a copy of any Help screen. You will print the current Help screen.

1. Be sure your printer is ready.
2. From the Help menu bar, select *PRINT*.

EXIT HELP

You can exit Help at any time by pressing Esc. When you exit Help, dBASE IV returns to the exact screen that was displayed when you asked for help. You will exit Help now to return to the Control Center.

Exit Help by pressing Esc.

*The Control Center is again displayed, with **<create>** highlighted in the Data panel.*

GET HELP WITH A SPECIFIC SCREEN

As you worked through this QUICK START, you used several dBASE IV screens: the Database Design screen, the Edit screen, the Browse screen, the Query Design screen, the Report Design screen, the Label Design screen, and the Form Design screen.

As you are using each of these screens, you can get help with the screen by pressing F1. You can also get help with any menu option at the top of the screen.

You will practice these procedures by getting help with the Browse screen and the Organize menu at the top of the Browse screen.

1. Open the Primary file.
2. Bring up the Browse screen by pressing F2.
3. Get help with the Browse screen:
   A. Bring up the Help screen by pressing F1.
   B. Read the Help information; when *<MORE F4>* is displayed, press F4 and read the next screen.
   C. When *<MORE F4>* is no longer displayed, exit Help by pressing Esc.
4. Get help with the Organize menu:
   A. Open the Organize menu.
   B. Highlight *Remove unwanted index tag*.
   C. Bring up the Help screen by pressing F1.
   D. Read the Help information.
   E. Exit Help by pressing Esc.
   F. Close the Organize menu by pressing Esc two times.
5. Return to the Control Center by opening the Exit menu and selecting *Exit*.

GET HELP WITH FILE MANAGEMENT

As you continue to work with dBASE IV, you will need to delete, copy, move, and rename files. The Tools menu includes options for performing these file management procedures. To preview these procedures, you will ask for help on each file management option.

1. At the Control Center, open the Tools menu.
2. Select *DOS utilities*.
3. Open the Operations menu.
4. Get help with the highlighted *Delete* option by pressing F1.
5. Read the Help screen for *Delete Files*.
6. Bring up the Help screen for Copy and Move (the next two Operations menu options) by pressing F4 (for the next screen).
7. Read the Help screen for *Copy or Move Files*.
8. Bring up the Help screen for Rename (the next Operations menu option) by pressing F4.
9. Read the Help screen for *Rename Files*.
10. Bring up next Help screen by pressing F4.
11. Read the Help screen for *Choose Files for Operation*.
12. Exit Help by pressing Esc.
13. Close the Operations menu by pressing Esc.
14. Return to the Control Center by opening the Exit menu and selecting *Exit to Control Center.*

COMPLETE SUPPLEMENTARY APPLICATION 20

For additional practice with the procedures covered in this lesson, complete Supplementary Application 20 on page 109. Use the lesson summary on the following page as needed.

BRING UP A HELP SCREEN   20A

Press F1

REVIEW THE HELP INFORMATION   20B

Read the first Help screen

When *<MORE F4>* is displayed at the end of a Help screen, press F4 to see the next screen

USE THE CONTENTS OPTION   20C

From the Help menu bar, select: *CONTENTS*

Select any desired topic

USE THE RELATED TOPICS OPTION   20D

From the Help menu bar, select: *RELATED TOPICS*

Select any desired topic

BACK UP TO THE PRECEDING HELP SCREEN   20E

From the Help menu bar, select: *BACKUP*

OR press F3

PRINT A HELP SCREEN   20F

Be sure your printer is ready

From the Help menu bar, select: *PRINT*

EXIT HELP   20G

Press Esc

GET HELP WITH A SPECIFIC SCREEN   20H

Display the screen (for example, the Browse screen, the Edit screen, the Report Design screen)

Press F1

GET HELP WITH FILE MANAGEMENT   20I

Open the Tools menu

Select: *DOS utilities*

Open the Operations menu

Highlight the option you want help with (Delete, Copy, Move, or Rename)

Press F1

APPENDIX *SUPPLEMENTARY APPLICATIONS*

• • • • • • • • • • • • • •

WIGGINS COLLECTION AGENCY

In the supplementary applications, you will be working for the Wiggins Collection Agency. Your company collects loans that are past due. With dBASE IV, you will maintain records on these loans, locate needed information from your files, and prepare reports as needed.

CREATING A CATALOG AND THE DATABASE FILE STRUCTURE

As you complete the following application, refer to the summary on page 16 as needed. The number preceding each instruction indicates the procedure being reviewed (for example, **1A** refers to Lesson **1**, Procedure **A**).

1A. Create and describe a catalog for the past-due loans:

        Catalog name: **COLLECT**

        Catalog description: **Past-due loans submitted for collection**

1B. Define the database file structure:

Field Name	Field Type	Width	Decimals	Index
LOAN_NO	Character	6		Y
LNAME	Character	10		N
FNAME	Character	8		N
DEFDATE	Date	8		N
AMOUNT	Numeric	10	2	N
SECURED	Logical	1		N

DEFDATE is the date that the borrower defaulted on the loan (that is, the date the loan was due but not paid). The SECURED field will indicate if the borrower put up collateral for the loan (that is, if the loan is backed up by other property).

1C. Review the file structure and correct any errors.

1D. Enter the file description: **Initial entering of past-due accounts**.

1E. Save the database file structure as **SETUP**.

1F. Exit dBASE IV.

ENTERING RECORDS INTO THE DATABASE FILE

As you complete the following application, refer to the summary on page 20 as needed.

Note: If you are continuing directly from Supplementary Application 1, you should exit and then restart dBASE IV now so that you can practice each of the procedures in this application.

2A. Open the Collect catalog.

2B. Enter the following records into the file. To enter the AMOUNT data, do not key the commas; also, when the amount is an even amount (for example, 10,000.00), you can key the whole number and the decimal (**10000.**) and dBASE IV will insert the two zeros after you press ⏎.

LOAN_NO	LNAME	FNAME	DEFDATE	AMOUNT	SECURED
567890	Tang	Felice	01/01/93	32,137.45	T
890123	Torris	Buck	03/16/92	10,000.00	F
456789	Rathabul	Jose	02/15/93	7,462.82	T
901234	Cooper	Cary	08/01/92	12,372.95	T
678990	DeFlowers	Susan	06/01/91	27,792.93	F
012345	Gruedecker	Hans	01/01/93	4,000.00	T
234567	Woodman	Cindy	01/01/93	10,000.00	T
789012	Helmut	Marcel	05/01/92	18,735.47	T
123456	Cooper	Marge	02/01/92	5,521.32	F

2C. Review the records and correct any errors.

2D. Save the records.

2E. Display the records on both the Edit screen and the Browse screen; then return to the Control Center.

2F. Print a Quick Report of the Setup file.

2G. Exit dBASE IV.

SUPPLEMENTARY APPLICATION 3:

EDITING THE DATABASE FILE

As you complete the following application, refer to the summary on page 24 as needed.

3A. With the Collect catalog open, display the records of the Setup file.

3B. Two additional loans were turned over to the company for collection. Add the records to the Setup file:

LOAN_NO	LNAME	FNAME	DEFDATE	AMOUNT	SECURED
678901	Watters	Mick	03/01/93	9,842.17	F
456789	Pov	Ster	03/25/93	7,140.00	F

3C. Buck Torris paid his account in full, and Jose Rathabul declared bankruptcy. Erase these two records from the file.

3D. Mark the DeFlowers record for deletion (see Summary, 3C); then unmark the record.

3E. Marcel Helmut paid $8,735.47 on his account. Therefore, change the loan amount to $10,000.

3F. Change Hans Gruedecker's first name to Shawn (see Summary, 3E); then undo the change.

3G. Save the edited file.

SORTING THE DATABASE FILE

As you complete the following application, refer to the summary on page 28 as needed.

4A. Open the Collect catalog. Then sort the Setup file to arrange the records in ascending numerical order by loan number (smallest numbers first). Save the sorted file as **ACCOUNTS**. Describe the file as **Defaulted loan information**.

4B. Open the new Accounts file and display the records. Observe that the records are sorted by loan number, smallest numbers first. Then return to the Control Center.

4C. Open the Setup file again and sort the records alphabetically by last name and then first name. Save the sorted file as **ACCTNAME**, and describe the file as **Accounts sorted by name**. Then display the records in the Acctname file (see Summary, 4B) and observe the order of the sorted records. Return to the Control Center.

4D. After reviewing the records in the two arrangements, you decide to maintain the database in numerical order by loan number (the Accounts file). Therefore, you will delete the Acctname and Setup files. First, close the Acctname file so that you can delete it in the next step.

4E. Delete the Acctname and Setup files.

CREATING AND USING INDEXES

As you complete the following application, refer to the summary on page 32 as needed.

5A. In the Collect catalog, display the records of the Accounts file.

The current records are sorted in numerical order by loan number. However, when you add new loans to the file, dBASE IV will list the new records at the end of the file—not in loan number order. You will often want to see all records in numerical order by loan number. Therefore, create an index on the LOAN_NO field; name the index NUMBER.

5B. Create a second index named NAME that will arrange the records alphabetically by last name and then first name.

5C. Create a third index named **DATE_AMT** that will arrange the records chronologically by default date (earliest dates first) and then by the loan amount (smallest amounts first). The index expression will be **DTOS(DEFDATE)+STR(AMOUNT)**.

5D. From the Browse screen, open the Name index and observe the record arrangement (alphabetical by name, ascending order; persons with the same last name are further arranged by first name). Then return to the Control Center.

From the Control Center, open the Date_Amt index. Then display the records to observe the record arrangement (chronological by default date; records which defaulted on the same date are listed numerically by amount, smallest amounts first). Return to the Control Center.

5E. Close the Date_Amt index by opening the Natural Order index from the Control Center. Display the records to observe the record arrangement (numerical by Loan Numbers, as the records appear in the sorted file). Return to the Control Center.

SUPPLEMENTARY APPLICATION 6:

MOVING AROUND IN THE FILE AND SEARCHING FOR INFORMATION

As you complete the following application, refer to the summary on page 36 as needed.

6A. With the Collect catalog open, display the records of the Accounts file. Move directly to the last record in the file (Cary Cooper). Then move directly to the top record in the file (Gruedecker).

6B. Skip five records to move to Record 6 (Watters).

6C. Move directly to Record 3 (Woodman).

6D. Perform a forward search for the first loan that has a default date of January 1, 1993 (the search string is **01/01/93**, including the diagonals). The first loan to match the search string is Tang. Locate the next loans of the same date by pressing SHIFT-F4 (Gruedecker and then Woodman).

6E. Perform a forward search for all loans which defaulted in 1992 (the search string is ***92**). You will find Helmut, then Cary Cooper, and finally Marge Cooper.

6F. Open the Number index. Perform an index search for loan number **678901** (Watters). Then return to the Control Center.

SUPPLEMENTARY APPLICATION 7:

SELECTING RECORDS BY CHARACTER DATA

As you complete the following application, refer to the summary on page 40 as needed.

7A. Open the Collect catalog and then open the Accounts file.

7B. Bring up the Query Design screen.

7C. Select the records of loans defaulted by persons named **Cooper**.

7D. Return to the Query Design screen.

7E. Clear **Cooper** from the LNAME field.

7F. We received a letter from an individual concerning her/his loan, and the signature appeared to be Goodman. Because a search of the file did not locate a Goodman, search for a person whose last name is **like *man** (Woodman). Then return to the Query Design screen and clear the condition.

7G. The receptionist took a message and said "A Mr. Waters called." Again, a search of the file did not locate the name. Search for a person whose name **sounds like "Waters"** (Watters). Then return to the Query Design screen and clear the condition.

7H. Select the records of loans defaulted by persons other than Cary and Marge Cooper. Then return to the Query Design screen and clear the condition.

7I. Select the records of loans that have **45** as a part of the loan number. Then return to the Query Design screen.

7J. Return to the Control Center without saving the query.

SUPPLEMENTARY APPLICATION 8:

SELECTING RECORDS BY NUMERIC DATA, DATES, OR LOGICAL DATA

As you complete the following application, refer to the summary on page 44 as needed.

8A. In the Collect catalog, open the Accounts file and bring up the Query Design screen. Select the records of loans in the amount of $10,000 (Woodman and Helmut). Then return to the Query Design screen and clear the condition.

8B. Select the records of loans less than $10,000 (Gruedecker, Marge Cooper, Pov, and Watters). Then return to the Query Design screen and clear the condition.

8C. Select the records of loans defaulted on January 1, 1993 (Gruedecker, Woodman, and Tang). Then return to the Query Design screen and clear the condition.

8D. Select the records of loans defaulted since June 1, 1992 (Gruedecker, Woodman, Pov, Tang, Watters, and Cary Cooper). Then return to the Query Design screen and clear the condition.

8E. Select the records of loans that are secured by other assets (Gruedecker, Woodman, Tang, Helmut, and Cary Cooper). Then return to the Query Design screen, but do not clear the condition.

8F. Count the number of loans that are secured by other assets (5).

8G. From the view, return directly to the Control Center without saving the query.

SELECTING RECORDS USING MULTIPLE CONDITIONS AND SUMMARY CALCULATIONS

As you complete the following application, refer to the summary on page 48 as needed.

9A. From the Collect catalog, open the Accounts file and bring up the Query Design screen. Then select the records of loans that exceed $10,000 and are not secured (DeFlowers). Then return to the Query Design screen and clear the conditions.

9B. Select the records of loans between $5,000 and $10,000 (Marge Cooper, Pov, and Watters). Then return to the Query Design screen and clear the condition.

9C. Select the records of loans of $12,000 or more OR loans that defaulted before June 1, 1992 (Marge Cooper, before June 1, 1992; Tang, $12,000 or more; DeFlowers, before June 1, 1992 and $12,000 or more; Helmut, before June 1, 1992; Cary Cooper, $12,000 or more). Then return to the Query Design screen and clear the conditions.

9D. Calculate the sum of all loans that are secured ($68,510.40). Then return to the Query Design screen and clear the condition and summary operator.

9E. Calculate the average of all loans that are not secured and count the number of these loans (4 loans with an average of $12,574.11). Then return to the Control Center without saving the query.

CREATING AND USING QUERY FILES

As you complete the following application, refer to the summary on page 52 as needed.

10A. From the Collect catalog, open the Accounts file and begin a query.

10B. On the Query Design screen, select the records of all unsecured loans.

10C. On the Query Design screen, arrange the selected records by loan number by selecting the Number index.

10D. On the Query Design screen, select the following fields for the query: LOAN_N0, LNAME, FNAME, AMOUNT.

Display the query data (the view) and check the record selection (Marge Cooper, Pov, Watters, and DeFlowers); the record arrangement (ascending loan numbers); and the field selection and arrangement (LOAN_NO, LNAME, FNAME, AMOUNT).

10E. Return to the Query Design screen. Then describe the query as **Unsecured loans**. Finally, save the query file as **NON_SEC**.

10F. Display the Non_Sec query data from the Control Center.

10G.　Print a Quick Report of the Non_Sec query file.

10H.　Close the Non_Sec query file.

SUPPLEMENTARY APPLICATION 11:

CREATING A COLUMN REPORT FROM A QUICK LAYOUT

As you complete the following application, refer to the summary on page 56 as needed.

In this application, you will create the following column report for the Accounts file from a Quick Layout:

```
Current date

        DEFAULTED LOANS - NOT SECURED

LOAN_NO    LNAME        FNAME            AMOUNT

123456     Cooper       Marge           5521.32
456789     Pov          Ster            7140.00
678901     Watters      Mick            9842.17
678990     DeFlowers    Susan          27792.93
                        TOTAL          50296.42
```

11A.　Open the Collect catalog and the Non_Sec query file.

11B.　Begin a column report from a Quick Layout.

11C.　Insert and delete blank lines and text as follows:

　　1.　In the Page Header Band, delete the page number line.
　　2.　In the Page Header Band, insert five blank lines after the date.
　　3.　In the Page Header Band, enter the report title (Line 5, Column 6).
　　4.　In the Report Summary Band, insert TOTAL in Column 14.

11D.　Change the left margin to 10 spaces.

11E.　View the report on the screen.

11F.　Print the report from the Report Design screen.

11G.　Describe the report as **No collateral accounts** and name the report file **NO_COLL**.

CREATING A COLUMN REPORT FROM SCRATCH

As you complete the following application, refer to the summary on page 60 as needed.

In this application you will create the following column report from scratch:

```
Current date

                      TOTAL DUE FROM LOANS

DEFAULT DATE       LAST NAME      FIRST NAME   DEFAULT AMOUNT      TOTAL DUE

06/01/91           DeFlowers      Susan           27,792.93       30,572.22
02/01/92           Cooper         Marge            5,521.32        6,073.45
05/01/92           Helmut         Marcel          10,000.00       11,000.00
08/01/92           Cooper         Cary            12,372.95       13,610.25
01/01/93           Gruedecker     Hans             4,000.00        4,400.00
01/01/93           Woodman        Cindy           10,000.00       11,000.00
01/01/93           Tang           Felice          32,137.45       35,351.20
03/01/93           Watters        Mick             9,842.17       10,826.39
03/25/93           Pov            Ster             7,140.00        7,854.00
                                                  118,806.82      130,687.50
```

12A. Open the Collect catalog. For the Accounts file, open the Date_Amt index from the Control Center.

12B. Begin a column report from scratch.

12C. In the Page Header Band, insert the current date on Line 1, beginning in Column 5.

12D. In the Page Header Band, insert the report title and the column headings in the positions indicated:

Line 3, Column 32: **TOTAL DUE FROM LOANS**
Line 5, Column 5:   **DEFAULT DATE**
Line 5, Column 22: **LAST NAME**
Line 5, Column 36: **FIRST NAME**
Line 5, Column 50: **DEFAULT AMOUNT**
Line 5, Column 69: **TOTAL DUE**

12E. In the Detail Band, add the appropriate fields for the first four report columns (align the fields with the column headings). Change the template for the AMOUNT field to include a comma: **999,999.99**

Note: If you do not change the template for the AMOUNT field when you first add the field to the report, you can change the template at any time as follows: Move to the field in the Detail Band, open the Fields menu, select *Modify field*, select *Template*, change the template as desired, and press Ctrl-End.

12F. In the Detail Band, create a calculated field to add a 10% collection fee for all loans (AMOUNT x 110%):

Field name: **TOTAL_DUE**
Expression: **AMOUNT*1.1**
Template: **999,999.99**

12G. In the Report Summary Band, insert a summary calculation to sum (add) the AMOUNT and TOTAL DUE columns. For each sum, change the template to **999,999.99**.

12H. View the report on the screen.

12I. Describe the report as **Defaulted amount plus collection fees**. Then save the report file as **TOTAL_DUE**.

SUPPLEMENTARY APPLICATION 13:

CREATING A FORM REPORT FROM A QUICK LAYOUT

As you complete the following application, refer to the summary on page 64 as needed.

In this application, you will create the following form report for each loan that is not secured:

```
Page No.   1
Current date


            DEFAULTED LOANS—NOT SECURED

LOAN_NO    123456              AMOUNT        5521.32

FNAME      Marge               LNAME      Cooper
```

13A. Open the Collect catalog and the Non_Sec query.

13B. Begin a form report from a Quick Layout.

13C. In the Page Header Band, enter the report title on Line 6, Column 12; then press ↵ to open a blank line.

13D. Move the following fields to the positions indicated:

AMOUNT   Move the field name and data to Line 1, Column 29
LNAME   Move the field name and data to Line 3, Column 29

13E. So that each report will print on a separate page, delete the first blank line in the Detail Band (Ctrl-Y) and then change the page length to 14 lines.

13F. View the report on the screen. If the view shows that each report page includes more or less than one record, increase or decrease the page length until the pages end appropriately.

13G. Describe the report as **Defaulted loans that are not secured**. Then save the report file as **DEF_LOAN**.

13H. Print the report from the Control Center.

CREATING A MAILMERGE REPORT FROM A QUICK LAYOUT

As you complete the following application, refer to the summary on page 68 as needed.

In this application, you will prepare the following mailmerge report for each loan in the Accounts file:

```
TO:        (FNAME and LNAME fields from the Accounts file)

FROM:      Abdy Afzali, Account Manager

DATE:      March 25, 1994

SUBJECT:   Loan in Default

The payment of your loan is past due. It has been turned over to
our agency for collection.

To avoid any further credit actions, please remit (AMOUNT field) for
loan number (LOAN_NO field) within ten days.
```

14A. Open the Collect catalog and the Accounts file. Then begin a mailmerge report from a Quick Layout.

14B. Set the left margin at 1 inch and the right margin at 7.5 inches. Clear the tab setting preceding 2 inches and set a tab at 2 inches.

14C. Beginning on Line 6, enter the report heading: **TO: FROM: DATE: SUBJECT:** and the data following each subheading. For the FNAME and LNAME field data following **TO:**, create a calculated field that will appropriately connect the fields.

14D. Enter the first paragraph of the report.

14E. Enter the second paragraph, adding the AMOUNT and LOAN_NO fields from the database file in the positions shown.

14F. Change the report subheadings (**TO: FROM: DATE: SUBJECT:**) to print in bold.

14G. View the reports on the screen.

14H. Print the reports. They will be printed in numeric order by loan number, which is the order of the records in the file.

14I.   Describe the report as **First contact with past-due accounts**. Then save the report file as **PAST_DUE**.

SUPPLEMENTARY APPLICATION 15:

MODIFYING THE FILE STRUCTURE AND ENTERING DATA INTO NEW FIELDS

As you complete the following application, refer to the summary on page 72 as needed.

15A.   Open the Collect catalog and retrieve the database file structure for the Accounts file.

15B.   Add the following new fields to the file:

Field Name	Field Type	Width	Decimals	Index
SUBDATE	Date			N
AGENT	Character	15		N
CLIENT	Character	15		N

The SUBDATE is the date the loan was submitted. The AGENT is the person assigned to collect the loan. The CLIENT is the company asking us to collect the loan.

15C.   Save the modified file structure.

15D.   Retrieve the Accounts file structure (see Summary, 15A), delete the DEFDATE field, and then save the modified file structure (see Summary, 15C).

15E.   Retrieve the Accounts file structure (see Summary, 15A), change the AGENT field width to 18 spaces, and then save the modified file structure (see Summary, 15C).

15F.   Freeze the SUBDATE field and then enter the dates as shown:

Gruedecker	**07/01/93**
Cooper, Marge	**08/01/92**
Woodman	**07/01/93**
Pov	**09/01/93**
Tang	**07/01/93**
Watters	**09/01/93**
DeFlowers	**12/01/91**
Helmut	**11/01/92**
Cooper, Cary	**02/01/93**

15G.   Freeze the AGENT field (see Summary, 15F) and then enter the following agents, using Shift-F8 for duplicate data: The agent for the first five records is **Crampton**; the agent for last four records is **Beard**.

15H.   Unfreeze the AGENT field.

15I.   Lock the LOAN_NO field. Then freeze the CLIENT field (see Summary, 15F) and enter the clients as shown:

Gruedecker	**First Federal**
Cooper, Marge	**Second National**

Woodman	**First Security**
Pov	**Second National**
Tang	**First Federal**
Watters	**Second National**
DeFlowers	**First Security**
Helmut	**First Security**
Cooper, Cary	**First Security**

15J. Unlock the LOAN_NO field.

l5K. Save the changed file.

SUPPLEMENTARY APPLICATION 16:

CREATING AND USING LINKED DATABASE FILES

As you complete the following application, refer to the summary on page 76 as needed.

16A. In the Collect catalog, create the following database file (see Summary, 1B):

Filename: ACCTADD
File description: Addresses of defaulted accounts

File structure:

Field Name	Field Type	Width	Decimals	Index
LOAN_NO	Character	6		Y
STREET	Character	20		N
CITY	Character	15		N
STATE	Character	2		N
ZIP	Character	5		Y

Describe and save the file structure (see Summary, 1D and 1E). Then enter the following records into the file (see Summary, 2B):

LOAN_NO	STREET	CITY	STATE	ZIP
012345	801 Elm	Memphis	TN	38101
123456	382 Ash	Haiti	MO	63850
234567	728 Oak	Cairo	IL	62914
456789	126 Hed	Morley	MO	63769
567890	823 Sea	Thebes	IL	62713
678901	237 Tan	Paris	TX	75640
678990	978 Fig	Osceola	AR	72370
789012	297 Gum	St. Louis	MO	63155
901234	934 Jam	Cuba	MO	63080

When you check your records, you will see that they are not in the order in which you entered them (numerical order by loan number). Instead, they are in ZIP order—the order of the last index you created in the file structure. When you create an index, the index remains active until you close the file, open a new index, or exit dBASE IV.

Save the completed file (see Summary, 2D).

16B.   Select the files to be linked (first the Accounts file, then the Acctadd file).

16C.   Link the files (the common field is LOAN_NO).

16D.   Describe the linked view as **Account addresses**. Then save the view as **LINK1**.

16E.   Begin the process of modifying the Link1 query file.

16F.   Select the following fields for the linked view: FNAME, LNAME, STREET, CITY, STATE, ZIP.

16G.   Select the records of persons living in Missouri (STATE = "MO") who have not secured their loans (SECURED = .F.).

16H.   Select the ZIP index for the query so that the records will be arranged numerically by ZIP code.

16I.   Apply the query. The records of Marge Cooper and Pov should be displayed, showing only their names and addresses. Save the modified query.

SUPPLEMENTARY APPLICATION 17:

CREATING LABELS

As you complete the following application, refer to the summary on page 80 as needed.

17A.   In the Collect catalog, open the Link1 query file. Then begin a label file.

17B.   Change the label selection to **15/16 x 3 1/2 by 2.**

17C.   Change the left margin of the labels to one-half inch.

17D.   On Line 1 in Column 5, create a calculated field to insert the FNAME and LNAME field data appropriately. Use the following calculation expression: **TRIM(FNAME)+" "+LNAME**.

Move down to Line 3 and create a calculated field to insert the CITY, STATE, and ZIP field data appropriately. Use the following calculation expression: **TRIM(CITY)+", "+STATE+" "+ZIP**.

17E.   Move back up to Line 2, Column 5, and add the STREET field.

17F.   View the labels on the screen.

17G.   Describe the label file as **Missouri accounts with no collateral** and then save the file as **NO_COLL**.

WORKING WITH MEMO FIELDS

As you complete the following application, refer to the summary on page 84 as needed.

18A. Open the Collect catalog and modify the Accounts file structure (see Summary, 15A) to include the following memo field as Field 7 (see Summary, 15B):

Field Name	Field Type	Width	Decimals	Index
COLLATERAL	Memo	10		N

Save the modified file structure (see Summary, 15C).

18B. You will use the COLLATERAL field to describe the property that was used to secure the loan. Display the records, freeze the Collateral field (see Summary, 15F), and enter the following collateral—do not press ↵ at the end of the data or you will be adding a blank line to the file.

Gruedecker:	**1957 Gibson Flying V Guitar**
Woodman:	**1989 Oldsmobile Toronado, VIN 834738294023**
Tang:	**1990 Fleetwood Mobile Home**
Helmut:	**1990 ZCraft Ski Boat, ID 23837**
Cooper, Cary:	**1992 Mazda RX-7, VIN 7382432913332**

Save the changed file.

18C. Create the following column report from scratch.

Tips: All records of the Accounts file are included; therefore, you need no query file.

The records are arranged by loan number (the natural order); therefore, you need no index.

The left margin is 1 inch; the right margin is 7.5 inches.

The title and field headings are part of the Page Header Band.

For the Detail Band, the LOAN_NO field begins in Column 10; the COLLATERAL field begins in Column 40.

To insert a blank line between records, press Ctrl-N at the end of the fields in the Detail Band to open the next line.

To make the memo field fit the report margins, size the memo data in the Detail Band.

```
                     COLLATERAL REPORT

     LOAN NUMBER                    COLLATERAL

     012345                  1957 Gibson Flying V Guitar

     123456

     234567                  1989 Oldsmobile Toronado, VIN
                             834738294023

     456789

     567890                  1990 Fleetwood Mobile Home

     678901

     678990

     789012                   1990 ZCraft Ski Boat, ID 23837

     901234                   1992 Mazda RX-7, VIN 7382432913332
```

View the report on the screen (see Summary, 12H). Describe the report as **Number and collateral** and save it as **COLLAT** (see Summary, 12I).

18D.   Display the records in the Accounts file and then add the following collateral to Helmut's loan: **1993 Honda Jet Ski**. Resave the changed file.

SUPPLEMENTARY APPLICATION 19:

CREATING A FORM FOR DATA ENTRY OR EDITING

As you complete the following application, refer to the summary on page 88 as needed.

In this application you will create the following form for the Accounts file. You will use the form each time you need to change a loan amount:

```
        ┌──────────────────────────────────────────────┐
        │                                              │
        │        FORM FOR CHANGING LOAN AMOUNTS        │
        │                                              │
        └──────────────────────────────────────────────┘

     LOAN NUMBER:   XXXXXX         LOAN AMOUNT:   9999999.99
```

19A.   Open the Collect catalog and the Accounts file. Then begin a form file from scratch.

19B. Create a box for the title of the form:

Upper-left corner of box: Row 3, Column 16
Lower-left corner of box: Row 7, Column 56

Move into the box and key the title.

19C. On Row 10, enter the field headings and fields in the following positions:

Column 10: **LOAN NUMBER:**
Column 24: The LOAN_NO field data
Column 40: **LOAN AMOUNT:**
Column 54: The AMOUNT field data

19D. Prevent the LOAN_NO field from being edited.

19E. Save the form as **EDIT_AMT**.

19F. Use the form to reduce the amount of the following loans (subtract the payments from the current loan amount and record the new loan amount).

Loan Number	Payment
012345	1000.00
456789	140.00

19G. Display the original Edit screen and then switch to the original Browse screen. Change Susan DeFlowers last name to Smith. Then save the edited file.

SUPPLEMENTARY APPLICATION 20:

GETTING HELP WITH dBASE IV

As you complete the following application, refer to the summary on page 92 as needed.

20A. At the Control Center, move the highlighting to any filename. Then bring up the Help screen by pressing F1.

20B. Review the Help information for *How to Use Files from the Control Center*.

20C. From the Help menu bar, select *CONTENTS*. Then select *How to Create and Delete Control Center Files*. Review the Help information.

20D. From the Help menu bar, select *RELATED TOPICS*. Then select *About the Control Center*. Review the Help information, pressing F4 each time <MORE F4> is displayed.

20E. Back up to the previous screen by selecting *BACKUP* from the Help menu bar. Then back up to the previous screen by pressing the F3 key.

20F. Print the Help screen *About the Control Center*.

20G. Exit Help.

20H. Get Help with the Form Design screen:

    1.   From the Forms panel, select *<create>*.
    2.   Close the Layout menu by pressing Esc.
    3.   Bring up the Help screen by pressing F1.
    4.   Review the Help information for *Design a Form*.
    5.   Exit Help.
    6.   Return to the Control Center by opening the Exit menu and selecting *Abandon changes and exit*.

20I. Get Help with adding files to the current catalog:

    1.   Open the Catalog menu.
    2.   Select *Add file to catalog*.
    3.   Bring up the Help screen.
    4.   Review the Help information for *Add Files to Catalog*.
    5.   Exit Help.
    6.   Return to the Control Center by pressing Esc two times.

INDEX

U

V

W